BiModal IT
Complete Self-Assessment Gui

The guidance in this Self-Assessment is
practices and standards in business pro
quality management. The guidance is a
judgment of the individual collaborators listed in the Acknowledgments.

Notice of rights

Trademarks

Table of Contents

About The Art of Service

The Art of Service, Business Process Architects since 2000, is dedicated to helping stakeholders achieve excellence.

Defining, designing, creating, and implementing a process to solve a stakeholders challenge or meet an objective is the most valuable role… In EVERY group, company, organization and department.

Unless you're talking a one-time, single-use project, there should be a process. Whether that process is managed and implemented by humans, AI, or a combination of the two, it needs to be designed by someone with a complex enough perspective to ask the right questions.

Someone capable of asking the right questions and step back and say, 'What are we really trying to accomplish here? And is there a different way to look at it?'

With The Art of Service's Standard Requirements Self-Assessments, we empower people who can do just that — whether their title is marketer, entrepreneur, manager, salesperson, consultant, Business Process Manager, executive assistant, IT Manager, CIO etc... —they are the people who rule the future. They are people who watch the process as it happens, and ask the right questions to make the process work better.

Contact us when you need any support with this Self-Assessment and any help with templates, blue-prints and examples of standard documents you might need:

http://theartofservice.com
service@theartofservice.com

Acknowledgments

This checklist was developed under the auspices of The Art of Service, chaired by Gerardus Blokdyk.

Representatives from several client companies participated in the preparation of this Self-Assessment.

In addition, we are thankful for the design and printing services provided.

Included Resources - how to access

Included with your purchase of the book is the BiModal IT Self-Assessment Spreadsheet Dashboard which contains all questions and Self-Assessment areas and auto-generates insights, graphs, and project RACI planning - all with examples to get you started right away.

How? Simply send an email to
access@theartofservice.com
with this books' title in the subject to get the BiModal IT Self Assessment Tool right away.

You will receive the following contents with New and Updated specific criteria:

- The latest quick edition of the book in PDF

- The latest complete edition of the book in PDF, which criteria correspond to the criteria in...

- The Self-Assessment Excel Dashboard, and...

- Example pre-filled Self-Assessment Excel Dashboard to get familiar with results generation

- In-depth specific Checklists covering the topic

- Project management checklists and templates to assist with implementation

INCLUDES LIFETIME SELF ASSESSMENT UPDATES

Every self assessment comes with Lifetime Updates and Lifetime Free Updated Books. Lifetime Updates is an industry-first feature which allows you to receive verified self assessment updates, ensuring you always have the most accurate information at your fingertips.

Get it now- you will be glad you did - do it now, before you forget.

Send an email to **access@theartofservice.com** with this books' title in the subject to get the BiModal IT Self Assessment Tool right away.

Your feedback is invaluable to us

If you recently bought this book, we would love to hear from you!
You can do this by writing a review on amazon (or the online store
where you purchased this book) about your last purchase! As part
of our continual service improvement process, we love to hear real
client experiences and feedback.

How does it work?
To post a review on Amazon, just log in to your account and click
on the Create Your Own Review button (under Customer Reviews)
of the relevant product page. You can find examples of product
reviews in Amazon. If you purchased from another online store,
simply follow their procedures.

What happens when I submit my review?
Once you have submitted your review, send us an email at
review@theartofservice.com with the link to your review so we
can properly thank you for your feedback.

Purpose of this Self-Assessment

This Self-Assessment has been developed to improve
understanding of the requirements and elements of BiModal
IT, based on best practices and standards in business process
architecture, design and quality management.

It is designed to allow for a rapid Self-Assessment to determine
how closely existing management practices and procedures
correspond to the elements of the Self-Assessment.

The criteria of requirements and elements of BiModal IT have been
rephrased in the format of a Self-Assessment questionnaire, with a
seven-criterion scoring system, as explained in this document.

In this format, even with limited background knowledge of
BiModal IT, a manager can quickly review existing operations

to determine how they measure up to the standards. This in turn can serve as the starting point of a 'gap analysis' to identify management tools or system elements that might usefully be implemented in the organization to help improve overall performance.

How to use the Self-Assessment

On the following pages are a series of questions to identify to what extent your BiModal IT initiative is complete in comparison to the requirements set in standards.

To facilitate answering the questions, there is a space in front of each question to enter a score on a scale of '1' to '5'.

1 Strongly Disagree

2 Disagree

3 Neutral

4 Agree

5 Strongly Agree

Read the question and rate it with the following in front of mind:

'In my belief, the answer to this question is clearly defined'.

There are two ways in which you can choose to interpret this statement;
1. how aware are you that the answer to the question is clearly defined
2. for more in-depth analysis you can choose to gather evidence and confirm the answer to the question. This

obviously will take more time, most Self-Assessment users opt for the first way to interpret the question and dig deeper later on based on the outcome of the overall Self-Assessment.

A score of '1' would mean that the answer is not clear at all, where a '5' would mean the answer is crystal clear and defined. Leave emtpy when the question is not applicable or you don't want to answer it, you can skip it without affecting your score. Write your score in the space provided.

After you have responded to all the appropriate statements in each section, compute your average score for that section, using the formula provided, and round to the nearest tenth. Then transfer to the corresponding spoke in the BiModal IT Scorecard on the second next page of the Self-Assessment.

Your completed BiModal IT Scorecard will give you a clear presentation of which BiModal IT areas need attention.

BiModal IT
Scorecard Example

Example of how the finalized Scorecard can look like:

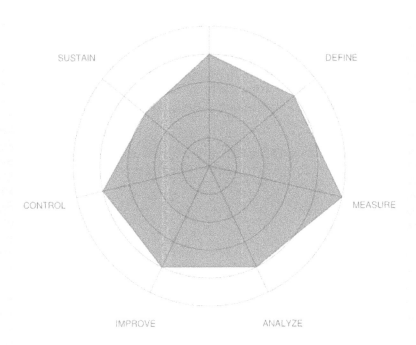

BiModal IT Scorecard

Your Scores:

BEGINNING OF THE SELF-ASSESSMENT:

CRITERION #1: RECOGNIZE

INTENT: Be aware of the need for change. Recognize that there is an unfavorable variation, problem or symptom.

In my belief, the answer to this question is clearly defined:

5 Strongly Agree

4 Agree

3 Neutral

2 Disagree

1 Strongly Disagree

1. Looking at each person individually – does every one have the qualities which are needed to work in this group?
<--- Score

2. To what extent would your organization benefit from being recognized as a award recipient?
<--- Score

3. What information do users need?
<--- Score

4. Who needs what information?
<--- Score

5. When a biModal IT manager recognizes a problem, what options are available?
<--- Score

6. How do you take a forward-looking perspective in identifying biModal IT research related to market response and models?
<--- Score

7. What would happen if biModal IT weren't done?
<--- Score

8. Who had the original idea?
<--- Score

9. Does your organization need more biModal IT education?
<--- Score

10. Who needs to know about biModal IT?
<--- Score

11. For your biModal IT project, identify and describe the business environment, is there more than one layer to the business environment?
<--- Score

12. How are you going to measure success?
<--- Score

13. Do you have/need 24-hour access to key personnel?
<--- Score

14. Are there any specific expectations or concerns about the biModal IT team, biModal IT itself?
<--- Score

15. What is the problem or issue?
<--- Score

16. How can auditing be a preventative security measure?
<--- Score

17. Are there any revenue recognition issues?
<--- Score

18. Are your goals realistic? Do you need to redefine your problem? Perhaps the problem has changed or maybe you have reached your goal and need to set a new one?
<--- Score

19. What are the business objectives to be achieved with biModal IT?
<--- Score

20. Think about the people you identified for your biModal IT project and the project responsibilities you would assign to them. what kind of training do you think they would need to perform these responsibilities effectively?
<--- Score

21. Who defines the rules in relation to any given

issue?

<--- Score

22. Is it clear when you think of the day ahead of you what activities and tasks you need to complete?

<--- Score

23. What are the minority interests and what amount of minority interests can be recognized?

<--- Score

24. What does biModal IT success mean to the stakeholders?

<--- Score

25. Will biModal IT deliverables need to be tested and, if so, by whom?

<--- Score

26. Does biModal IT create potential expectations in other areas that need to be recognized and considered?

<--- Score

27. Do you need to avoid or amend any biModal IT activities?

<--- Score

28. How do you identify the kinds of information that you will need?

<--- Score

29. What needs to be done?

<--- Score

30. How are the biModal IT's objectives aligned to the

organization's overall business strategy?
<--- Score

31. Who are your key stakeholders who need to sign off?
<--- Score

32. Will it solve real problems?
<--- Score

33. Are there recognized biModal IT problems?
<--- Score

34. Are controls defined to recognize and contain problems?
<--- Score

35. How do you assess your biModal IT workforce capability and capacity needs, including skills, competencies, and staffing levels?
<--- Score

36. What do you need to start doing?
<--- Score

37. What vendors make products that address the biModal IT needs?
<--- Score

38. Consider your own biModal IT project, what types of organizational problems do you think might be causing or affecting your problem, based on the work done so far?
<--- Score

39. How does it fit into your organizational needs and

tasks?
<--- Score

40. Do you know what you need to know about biModal IT?
<--- Score

41. Are you dealing with any of the same issues today as yesterday? What can you do about this?
<--- Score

42. Are there biModal IT problems defined?
<--- Score

43. As a sponsor, customer or management, how important is it to meet goals, objectives?
<--- Score

44. What should be considered when identifying available resources, constraints, and deadlines?
<--- Score

45. What are your needs in relation to biModal IT skills, labor, equipment, and markets?
<--- Score

46. What problems are you facing and how do you consider biModal IT will circumvent those obstacles?
<--- Score

47. To what extent does each concerned units management team recognize biModal IT as an effective investment?
<--- Score

48. Should you invest in industry-recognized

qualications?

<--- Score

49. What extra resources will you need?

<--- Score

50. What kind of organization model you would need?

<--- Score

51. What are the expected benefits of biModal IT to the business?

<--- Score

52. What else needs to be measured?

<--- Score

53. What is the smallest subset of the problem you can usefully solve?

<--- Score

54. What are the timeframes required to resolve each of the issues/problems?

<--- Score

55. Can management personnel recognize the monetary benefit of biModal IT?

<--- Score

56. Will new equipment/products be required to facilitate biModal IT delivery, for example is new software needed?

<--- Score

57. Do you need different information or graphics?

<--- Score

58. What tools and technologies are needed for a custom biModal IT project?
<--- Score

59. What prevents you from making the changes you know will make you a more effective biModal IT leader?
<--- Score

60. What training and capacity building actions are needed to implement proposed reforms?
<--- Score

61. How much are sponsors, customers, partners, stakeholders involved in biModal IT? In other words, what are the risks, if biModal IT does not deliver successfully?
<--- Score

62. Who else hopes to benefit from it?
<--- Score

63. What situation(s) led to this biModal IT Self Assessment?
<--- Score

64. Are problem definition and motivation clearly presented?
<--- Score

65. Will a response program recognize when a crisis occurs and provide some level of response?
<--- Score

Add up total points for this section:

_____ = Total points for this section

Divided by: _____ (number of
statements answered) = _____
Average score for this section

Transfer your score to the biModal IT
Index at the beginning of the Self-
Assessment.

CRITERION #2: DEFINE:

INTENT: Formulate the business problem. Define the problem, needs and objectives.

In my belief, the answer to this question is clearly defined:

5 Strongly Agree

4 Agree

3 Neutral

2 Disagree

1 Strongly Disagree

1. Are business processes mapped?
<--- Score

2. When are meeting minutes sent out? Who is on the distribution list?
<--- Score

3. Is full participation by members in regularly held team meetings guaranteed?

<--- Score

4. What are the Roles and Responsibilities for each team member and its leadership? Where is this documented?
<--- Score

5. How do you gather biModal IT requirements?
<--- Score

6. What system do you use for gathering biModal IT information?
<--- Score

7. Has a high-level 'as is' process map been completed, verified and validated?
<--- Score

8. Are there any constraints known that bear on the ability to perform biModal IT work? How is the team addressing them?
<--- Score

9. How do you manage scope?
<--- Score

10. What critical content must be communicated – who, what, when, where, and how?
<--- Score

11. Has everyone on the team, including the team leaders, been properly trained?
<--- Score

12. How often are the team meetings?
<--- Score

13. Who is gathering biModal IT information?
<--- Score

14. Are different versions of process maps needed to account for the different types of inputs?
<--- Score

15. When was the biModal IT start date?
<--- Score

16. Has the direction changed at all during the course of biModal IT? If so, when did it change and why?
<--- Score

17. Is a fully trained team formed, supported, and committed to work on the biModal IT improvements?
<--- Score

18. What is the scope of biModal IT?
<--- Score

19. Is biModal IT currently on schedule according to the plan?
<--- Score

20. What is the scope?
<--- Score

21. When is the estimated completion date?
<--- Score

22. What specifically is the problem? Where does it occur? When does it occur? What is its extent?
<--- Score

23. Is it clearly defined in and to your organization what you do?
<--- Score

24. How was the 'as is' process map developed, reviewed, verified and validated?
<--- Score

25. Will team members perform biModal IT work when assigned and in a timely fashion?
<--- Score

26. Do the problem and goal statements meet the SMART criteria (specific, measurable, attainable, relevant, and time-bound)?
<--- Score

27. How does the biModal IT manager ensure against scope creep?
<--- Score

28. How do you think the partners involved in biModal IT would have defined success?
<--- Score

29. What is the scope of the biModal IT effort?
<--- Score

30. Does the scope remain the same?
<--- Score

31. What biModal IT requirements should be gathered?
<--- Score

32. Is data collected and displayed to better

understand customer(s) critical needs and requirements.
<--- Score

33. What is the definition of success?
<--- Score

34. Has a project plan, Gantt chart, or similar been developed/completed?
<--- Score

35. Is there a critical path to deliver biModal IT results?
<--- Score

36. Have all basic functions of biModal IT been defined?
<--- Score

37. How would you define the culture at your organization, how susceptible is it to biModal IT changes?
<--- Score

38. What is out of scope?
<--- Score

39. Is the team formed and are team leaders (Coaches and Management Leads) assigned?
<--- Score

40. Is the current 'as is' process being followed? If not, what are the discrepancies?
<--- Score

41. Is the biModal IT scope manageable?
<--- Score

42. What key business process output measure(s) does biModal IT leverage and how?
<--- Score

43. What is in scope?
<--- Score

44. What are the record-keeping requirements of biModal IT activities?
<--- Score

45. Is the improvement team aware of the different versions of a process: what they think it is vs. what it actually is vs. what it should be vs. what it could be?
<--- Score

46. Is biModal IT linked to key business goals and objectives?
<--- Score

47. What customer feedback methods were used to solicit their input?
<--- Score

48. Is the biModal IT scope complete and appropriately sized?
<--- Score

49. How is the team tracking and documenting its work?
<--- Score

50. What defines best in class?
<--- Score

51. Is biModal IT required?
<--- Score

52. How will the biModal IT team and the organization measure complete success of biModal IT?
<--- Score

53. Is there a biModal IT management charter, including business case, problem and goal statements, scope, milestones, roles and responsibilities, communication plan?
<--- Score

54. Have specific policy objectives been defined?
<--- Score

55. If substitutes have been appointed, have they been briefed on the biModal IT goals and received regular communications as to the progress to date?
<--- Score

56. Is there regularly 100% attendance at the team meetings? If not, have appointed substitutes attended to preserve cross-functionality and full representation?
<--- Score

57. What are the dynamics of the communication plan?
<--- Score

58. How did the biModal IT manager receive input to the development of a biModal IT improvement plan and the estimated completion dates/times of each activity?
<--- Score

59. Is the team adequately staffed with the desired cross-functionality? If not, what additional resources are available to the team?
<--- Score

60. How will variation in the actual durations of each activity be dealt with to ensure that the expected biModal IT results are met?
<--- Score

61. Who defines (or who defined) the rules and roles?
<--- Score

62. Is there a completed, verified, and validated high-level 'as is' (not 'should be' or 'could be') business process map?
<--- Score

63. What are the rough order estimates on cost savings/opportunities that biModal IT brings?
<--- Score

64. Has your scope been defined?
<--- Score

65. How do you hand over biModal IT context?
<--- Score

66. What happens if biModal IT's scope changes?
<--- Score

67. What is the context?
<--- Score

68. Who are the biModal IT improvement team

members, including Management Leads and Coaches?
<--- Score

69. Has the biModal IT work been fairly and/or equitably divided and delegated among team members who are qualified and capable to perform the work? Has everyone contributed?
<--- Score

70. How and when will the baselines be defined?
<--- Score

71. How can the value of biModal IT be defined?
<--- Score

72. Have the customer needs been translated into specific, measurable requirements? How?
<--- Score

73. What baselines are required to be defined and managed?
<--- Score

74. What are the tasks and definitions?
<--- Score

75. Is the scope of biModal IT defined?
<--- Score

76. What constraints exist that might impact the team?
<--- Score

77. Has anyone else (internal or external to the organization) attempted to solve this problem or

a similar one before? If so, what knowledge can be leveraged from these previous efforts?
<--- Score

78. What are the boundaries of the scope? What is in bounds and what is not? What is the start point? What is the stop point?
<--- Score

79. Are resources adequate for the scope?
<--- Score

80. Is the team sponsored by a champion or business leader?
<--- Score

81. Are task requirements clearly defined?
<--- Score

82. What are the compelling business reasons for embarking on biModal IT?
<--- Score

83. What is out-of-scope initially?
<--- Score

84. Are customer(s) identified and segmented according to their different needs and requirements?
<--- Score

85. How do you keep key subject matter experts in the loop?
<--- Score

86. Are required metrics defined, what are they?
<--- Score

87. Is scope creep really all bad news?
<--- Score

88. Are there different segments of customers?
<--- Score

89. In what way can you redefine the criteria of choice clients have in your category in your favor?
<--- Score

90. Are accountability and ownership for biModal IT clearly defined?
<--- Score

91. What would be the goal or target for a biModal IT's improvement team?
<--- Score

92. What is in the scope and what is not in scope?
<--- Score

93. What was the context?
<--- Score

94. Have all of the relationships been defined properly?
<--- Score

95. What sources do you use to gather information for a biModal IT study?
<--- Score

96. Is there a completed SIPOC representation, describing the Suppliers, Inputs, Process, Outputs, and Customers?

<--- Score

97. Are team charters developed?
<--- Score

98. Are audit criteria, scope, frequency and methods defined?
<--- Score

99. Are roles and responsibilities formally defined?
<--- Score

100. Are customers identified and high impact areas defined?
<--- Score

101. What scope to assess?
<--- Score

102. Do you all define biModal IT in the same way?
<--- Score

103. Does the team have regular meetings?
<--- Score

104. Are approval levels defined for contracts and supplements to contracts?
<--- Score

105. Are improvement team members fully trained on biModal IT?
<--- Score

106. Has the improvement team collected the 'voice of the customer' (obtained feedback – qualitative and quantitative)?

<--- Score

107. Why are you doing biModal IT and what is the scope?
<--- Score

108. Is the team equipped with available and reliable resources?
<--- Score

109. Will team members regularly document their biModal IT work?
<--- Score

110. Scope of sensitive information?
<--- Score

111. Should the organization be required to build a redundant, parallel system or share common infrastructure?
<--- Score

112. Has a team charter been developed and communicated?
<--- Score

113. Has/have the customer(s) been identified?
<--- Score

Add up total points for this section:
_ _ _ _ _ = Total points for this section

Divided by: _ _ _ _ _ _ (number of statements answered) = _ _ _ _ _ _
Average score for this section

Transfer your score to the biModal IT
Index at the beginning of the Self-
Assessment.

CRITERION #3: MEASURE:

INTENT: Gather the correct data.
Measure the current performance and
evolution of the situation.

In my belief, the answer to this
question is clearly defined:

5 Strongly Agree

4 Agree

3 Neutral

2 Disagree

1 Strongly Disagree

1. Do staff have the necessary skills to collect, analyze, and report data?
<--- Score

2. What could cause you to change course?
<--- Score

3. Which stakeholder characteristics are analyzed?
<--- Score

4. Does biModal IT analysis show the relationships among important biModal IT factors?
<--- Score

5. Have you found any 'ground fruit' or 'low-hanging fruit' for immediate remedies to the gap in performance?
<--- Score

6. What are the uncertainties surrounding estimates of impact?
<--- Score

7. Does your organization systematically track and analyze outcomes related for accountability and quality improvement?
<--- Score

8. What harm might be caused?
<--- Score

9. Are there measurements based on task performance?
<--- Score

10. Is there a Performance Baseline?
<--- Score

11. What are your key biModal IT indicators that you will measure, analyze and track?
<--- Score

12. How will your organization measure success?
<--- Score

13. What is measured? Why?
<--- Score

14. How do you know that any biModal IT analysis is complete and comprehensive?
<--- Score

15. What causes mismanagement?
<--- Score

16. Among the biModal IT product and service cost to be estimated, which is considered hardest to estimate?
<--- Score

17. How much will the redevelopment cost?
<--- Score

18. Does biModal IT systematically track and analyze outcomes for accountability and quality improvement?
<--- Score

19. Who participated in the data collection for measurements?
<--- Score

20. Are the units of measure consistent?
<--- Score

21. Is data collection planned and executed?
<--- Score

22. What are the types and number of measures to use?
<--- Score

23. Is it possible to estimate the impact of unanticipated complexity such as wrong or failed assumptions, feedback, etc. on proposed reforms?
<--- Score

24. How is performance measured?
<--- Score

25. What methods are feasible and acceptable to estimate the impact of reforms?
<--- Score

26. How frequently do you track biModal IT measures?
<--- Score

27. Are the measurements objective?
<--- Score

28. How can you measure the performance?
<--- Score

29. How do you aggregate measures across priorities?
<--- Score

30. Are you taking your company in the direction of better and revenue or cheaper and cost?
<--- Score

31. How do you measure progress and evaluate training effectiveness?
<--- Score

32. How will you measure success?
<--- Score

33. Is data collected on key measures that were identified?
<--- Score

34. How do you focus on what is right -not who is right?
<--- Score

35. How do you control the overall costs of your work processes?
<--- Score

36. How large is the gap between current performance and the customer-specified (goal) performance?
<--- Score

37. What charts has the team used to display the components of variation in the process?
<--- Score

38. The approach of traditional biModal IT works for detail complexity but is focused on a systematic approach rather than an understanding of the nature of systems themselves, what approach will permit your organization to deal with the kind of unpredictable emergent behaviors that dynamic complexity can introduce?
<--- Score

39. Are high impact defects defined and identified in the business process?
<--- Score

40. Is Process Variation Displayed/Communicated?
<--- Score

41. How do you measure variability?
<--- Score

42. What is an unallowable cost?
<--- Score

43. Are missed biModal IT opportunities costing your organization money?
<--- Score

44. Who should receive measurement reports?
<--- Score

45. How is the value delivered by biModal IT being measured?
<--- Score

46. Is long term and short term variability accounted for?
<--- Score

47. How do you measure efficient delivery of biModal IT services?
<--- Score

48. How can you measure biModal IT in a systematic way?
<--- Score

49. What are the costs of reform?
<--- Score

50. How do you stay flexible and focused to recognize larger biModal IT results?
<--- Score

51. Have you made assumptions about the shape of the future, particularly its impact on your customers and competitors?
<--- Score

52. What are the agreed upon definitions of the high impact areas, defect(s), unit(s), and opportunities that will figure into the process capability metrics?
<--- Score

53. How do you measure success?
<--- Score

54. How do you measure lifecycle phases?
<--- Score

55. Do you aggressively reward and promote the people who have the biggest impact on creating excellent biModal IT services/products?
<--- Score

56. Have the types of risks that may impact biModal IT been identified and analyzed?
<--- Score

57. Why do the measurements/indicators matter?
<--- Score

58. Why do you expend time and effort to implement measurement, for whom?
<--- Score

59. Is a solid data collection plan established that includes measurement systems analysis?
<--- Score

60. What measurements are possible, practicable and meaningful?
<--- Score

61. What causes extra work or rework?
<--- Score

62. What data was collected (past, present, future/ ongoing)?
<--- Score

63. Is key measure data collection planned and executed, process variation displayed and communicated and performance baselined?
<--- Score

64. Can you measure the return on analysis?
<--- Score

65. Are process variation components displayed/ communicated using suitable charts, graphs, plots?
<--- Score

66. What measurements are being captured?
<--- Score

67. How do you do risk analysis of rare, cascading, catastrophic events?
<--- Score

68. What has the team done to assure the stability and accuracy of the measurement process?
<--- Score

69. What particular quality tools did the team find

helpful in establishing measurements?
<--- Score

70. How will success or failure be measured?
<--- Score

71. Was a data collection plan established?
<--- Score

72. Does biModal IT analysis isolate the fundamental causes of problems?
<--- Score

73. Is the solution cost-effective?
<--- Score

74. What key measures identified indicate the performance of the business process?
<--- Score

75. What disadvantage does this cause for the user?
<--- Score

76. How are measurements made?
<--- Score

77. Where is it measured?
<--- Score

78. Did you tackle the cause or the symptom?
<--- Score

79. Have changes been properly/adequately analyzed for effect?
<--- Score

80. Can you do biModal IT without complex (expensive) analysis?

<--- Score

81. Are key measures identified and agreed upon?

<--- Score

82. How is progress measured?

<--- Score

83. What could cause delays in the schedule?

<--- Score

84. What evidence is there and what is measured?

<--- Score

85. Have the concerns of stakeholders to help identify and define potential barriers been obtained and analyzed?

<--- Score

86. Are you aware of what could cause a problem?

<--- Score

87. Are losses documented, analyzed, and remedial processes developed to prevent future losses?

<--- Score

88. What do you measure and why?

<--- Score

89. How will measures be used to manage and adapt?

<--- Score

90. How do you identify and analyze stakeholders and their interests?

<--- Score

91. What are your key biModal IT organizational performance measures, including key short and longer-term financial measures?
<--- Score

92. How do your measurements capture actionable biModal IT information for use in exceeding your customers expectations and securing your customers engagement?
<--- Score

93. How does IT ambidexterity impact organizational agility?
<--- Score

94. Does the biModal IT task fit the client's priorities?
<--- Score

95. Do you effectively measure and reward individual and team performance?
<--- Score

96. How will effects be measured?
<--- Score

97. Is decentralization more cost effective?
<--- Score

98. What are the key input variables? What are the key process variables? What are the key output variables?
<--- Score

99. What would be a real cause for concern?
<--- Score

100. What is the right balance of time and resources between investigation, analysis, and discussion and dissemination?
<--- Score

101. What causes investor action?
<--- Score

102. How to cause the change?
<--- Score

103. What potential environmental factors impact the biModal IT effort?
<--- Score

104. What are your customers expectations and measures?
<--- Score

105. What relevant entities could be measured?
<--- Score

106. How will you measure your biModal IT effectiveness?
<--- Score

107. Which measures and indicators matter?
<--- Score

Add up total points for this section:
_ _ _ _ _ = Total points for this section

Divided by: _ _ _ _ _ _ (number of statements answered) = _ _ _ _ _ _ Average score for this section

Transfer your score to the biModal IT Index at the beginning of the Self-Assessment.

CRITERION #4: ANALYZE:

INTENT: Analyze causes, assumptions and hypotheses.

In my belief, the answer to this question is clearly defined:

5 Strongly Agree

4 Agree

3 Neutral

2 Disagree

1 Strongly Disagree

1. What are your key performance measures or indicators and in-process measures for the control and improvement of your biModal IT processes?
<--- Score

2. What quality tools were used to get through the analyze phase?
<--- Score

3. A compounding model resolution with available

relevant data can often provide insight towards a solution methodology; which biModal IT models, tools and techniques are necessary?
<--- Score

4. What were the financial benefits resulting from any 'ground fruit or low-hanging fruit' (quick fixes)?
<--- Score

5. How do mission and objectives affect the biModal IT processes of your organization?
<--- Score

6. How does the organization define, manage, and improve its biModal IT processes?
<--- Score

7. What does the data say about the performance of the business process?
<--- Score

8. Do your contracts/agreements contain data security obligations?
<--- Score

9. Is the required biModal IT data gathered?
<--- Score

10. Do your leaders quickly bounce back from setbacks?
<--- Score

11. Are gaps between current performance and the goal performance identified?
<--- Score

12. Do you, as a leader, bounce back quickly from setbacks?
<--- Score

13. Did any additional data need to be collected?
<--- Score

14. Was a cause-and-effect diagram used to explore the different types of causes (or sources of variation)?
<--- Score

15. What conclusions were drawn from the team's data collection and analysis? How did the team reach these conclusions?
<--- Score

16. How do you implement and manage your work processes to ensure that they meet design requirements?
<--- Score

17. What biModal IT data do you gather or use now?
<--- Score

18. What successful thing are you doing today that may be blinding you to new growth opportunities?
<--- Score

19. What did the team gain from developing a sub-process map?
<--- Score

20. Is the suppliers process defined and controlled?
<--- Score

21. How was the detailed process map generated,

verified, and validated?
<--- Score

22. What controls do you have in place to protect data?
<--- Score

23. What methods do you use to gather biModal IT data?
<--- Score

24. Do your employees have the opportunity to do what they do best everyday?
<--- Score

25. Was a detailed process map created to amplify critical steps of the 'as is' business process?
<--- Score

26. Do several people in different organizational units assist with the biModal IT process?
<--- Score

27. Were there any improvement opportunities identified from the process analysis?
<--- Score

28. Is the performance gap determined?
<--- Score

29. What are the best opportunities for value improvement?
<--- Score

30. How often will data be collected for measures?
<--- Score

31. What is your organizations process which leads to recognition of value generation?
<--- Score

32. What were the crucial 'moments of truth' on the process map?
<--- Score

33. What are your current levels and trends in key measures or indicators of biModal IT product and process performance that are important to and directly serve your customers? How do these results compare with the performance of your competitors and other organizations with similar offerings?
<--- Score

34. How do you drive bimodal IT and adaptive sourcing strategies?
<--- Score

35. What will drive biModal IT change?
<--- Score

36. What are your current levels and trends in key biModal IT measures or indicators of product and process performance that are important to and directly serve your customers?
<--- Score

37. How is the way you as the leader think and process information affecting your organizational culture?
<--- Score

38. Record-keeping requirements flow from the records needed as inputs, outputs, controls and

for transformation of a biModal IT process. Are the records needed as inputs to the biModal IT process available?
<--- Score

39. How do your work systems and key work processes relate to and capitalize on your core competencies?
<--- Score

40. What are your biModal IT processes?
<--- Score

41. How do you identify specific biModal IT investment opportunities and emerging trends?
<--- Score

42. Identify an operational issue in your organization. for example, could a particular task be done more quickly or more efficiently by biModal IT?
<--- Score

43. What data is gathered?
<--- Score

44. Were any designed experiments used to generate additional insight into the data analysis?
<--- Score

45. If your service goes down, do you know where the data resides and do you have access to a back-up?
<--- Score

46. Did any value-added analysis or 'lean thinking' take place to identify some of the gaps shown on the

'as is' process map?
<--- Score

47. Were Pareto charts (or similar) used to portray the 'heavy hitters' (or key sources of variation)?
<--- Score

48. What are your best practices for minimizing biModal IT project risk, while demonstrating incremental value and quick wins throughout the biModal IT project lifecycle?
<--- Score

49. What other organizational variables, such as reward systems or communication systems, affect the performance of this biModal IT process?
<--- Score

50. What tools were used to narrow the list of possible causes?
<--- Score

51. Have any additional benefits been identified that will result from closing all or most of the gaps?
<--- Score

52. What are the revised rough estimates of the financial savings/opportunity for biModal IT improvements?
<--- Score

53. Is Data and process analysis, root cause analysis and quantifying the gap/opportunity in place?
<--- Score

54. How is biModal IT data gathered?

<--- Score

55. Have the problem and goal statements been updated to reflect the additional knowledge gained from the analyze phase?
<--- Score

56. What is the cost of poor quality as supported by the team's analysis?
<--- Score

57. Think about the functions involved in your biModal IT project, what processes flow from these functions?
<--- Score

58. Where is the data coming from to measure compliance?
<--- Score

59. How do you promote understanding that opportunity for improvement is not criticism of the status quo, or the people who created the status quo?
<--- Score

60. What tools were used to generate the list of possible causes?
<--- Score

61. An organizationally feasible system request is one that considers the mission, goals and objectives of the organization. Key questions are: is the biModal IT solution request practical and will it solve a problem or take advantage of an opportunity to achieve company goals?
<--- Score

62. Is the gap/opportunity displayed and communicated in financial terms?
<--- Score

63. Think about some of the processes you undertake within your organization, which do you own?
<--- Score

64. Where is biModal IT data gathered?
<--- Score

65. What process should you select for improvement?
<--- Score

66. Is the biModal IT process severely broken such that a re-design is necessary?
<--- Score

67. What other jobs or tasks affect the performance of the steps in the biModal IT process?
<--- Score

68. Can you add value to the current biModal IT decision-making process (largely qualitative) by incorporating uncertainty modeling (more quantitative)?
<--- Score

69. Are biModal IT changes recognized early enough to be approved through the regular process?
<--- Score

Add up total points for this section:
_ _ _ _ _ = Total points for this section

Divided by: _____ (number of
statements answered) = _____
Average score for this section

Transfer your score to the biModal IT
Index at the beginning of the Self-
Assessment.

CRITERION #5: IMPROVE:

INTENT: Develop a practical solution.
Innovate, establish and test the
solution and to measure the results.

In my belief, the answer to this
question is clearly defined:

5 Strongly Agree

4 Agree

3 Neutral

2 Disagree

1 Strongly Disagree

1. For decision problems, how do you develop a
decision statement?
<--- Score

2. How do you measure improved biModal IT service
perception, and satisfaction?
<--- Score

3. What actually has to improve and by how much?

<--- Score

4. How will the team or the process owner(s) monitor the implementation plan to see that it is working as intended?
<--- Score

5. How will the organization know that the solution worked?
<--- Score

6. Who controls the risk?
<--- Score

7. What went well, what should change, what can improve?
<--- Score

8. Risk Identification: What are the possible risk events your organization faces in relation to biModal IT?
<--- Score

9. Are new and improved process ('should be') maps developed?
<--- Score

10. Is bimodal IT truly a new type of corporate IT structure for fostering innovation, or just a new label for the citizen development or shadow IT already existing in organizations?
<--- Score

11. How will you measure the results?
<--- Score

12. Risk events: what are the things that could go

wrong?

<--- Score

13. How do you go about comparing biModal IT approaches/solutions?

<--- Score

14. How much time will it take to complete redevelopment?

<--- Score

15. What communications are necessary to support the implementation of the solution?

<--- Score

16. What needs improvement? Why?

<--- Score

17. How will you know that you have improved?

<--- Score

18. Is there a high likelihood that any recommendations will achieve their intended results?

<--- Score

19. Is the optimal solution selected based on testing and analysis?

<--- Score

20. Do those selected for the biModal IT team have a good general understanding of what biModal IT is all about?

<--- Score

21. How do you maintain the consistency and protection of your environment when developers

**have operational access to infrastructure and
network configuration in the cloud?**
<--- Score

22. How do you manage and improve your biModal IT
work systems to deliver customer value and achieve
organizational success and sustainability?
<--- Score

23. Was a pilot designed for the proposed solution(s)?
<--- Score

24. How can skill-level changes improve biModal IT?
<--- Score

25. Is supporting biModal IT documentation required?
<--- Score

26. Are there any constraints (technical, political,
cultural, or otherwise) that would inhibit certain
solutions?
<--- Score

27. What attendant changes will need to be made to
ensure that the solution is successful?
<--- Score

28. Is the implementation plan designed?
<--- Score

29. What is biModal IT's impact on utilizing the best
solution(s)?
<--- Score

30. What does the 'should be' process map/design
look like?

<--- Score

31. How do the biModal IT results compare with the performance of your competitors and other organizations with similar offerings?
<--- Score

32. How will you know that a change is an improvement?
<--- Score

33. How significant is the improvement in the eyes of the end user?
<--- Score

34. What is the risk?
<--- Score

35. What practices helps your organization to develop its capacity to recognize patterns?
<--- Score

36. How do you improve biModal IT service perception, and satisfaction?
<--- Score

37. What improvements have been achieved?
<--- Score

38. What resources are required for the improvement efforts?
<--- Score

39. Are you assessing biModal IT and risk?
<--- Score

40. Are improved process ('should be') maps modified based on pilot data and analysis?
<--- Score

41. How did the team generate the list of possible solutions?
<--- Score

42. Which of the recognised risks out of all risks can be most likely transferred?
<--- Score

43. Who are the people involved in developing and implementing biModal IT?
<--- Score

44. Risk factors: what are the characteristics of biModal IT that make it risky?
<--- Score

45. What tools were used to evaluate the potential solutions?
<--- Score

46. What were the underlying assumptions on the cost-benefit analysis?
<--- Score

47. Are the original developers still with the organisation?
<--- Score

48. What can you do to improve?
<--- Score

49. What is the implementation plan?

<--- Score

50. How can you improve biModal IT?
<--- Score

51. Does the goal represent a desired result that can be measured?
<--- Score

52. How can you improve performance?
<--- Score

53. What tools were used to tap into the creativity and encourage 'outside the box' thinking?
<--- Score

54. What error proofing will be done to address some of the discrepancies observed in the 'as is' process?
<--- Score

55. When you map the key players in your own work and the types/domains of relationships with them, which relationships do you find easy and which challenging, and why?
<--- Score

56. How do you define the solutions' scope?
<--- Score

57. What are the implications of the one critical biModal IT decision 10 minutes, 10 months, and 10 years from now?
<--- Score

58. What tools were most useful during the improve phase?

<--- Score

59. Who will be responsible for making the decisions to include or exclude requested changes once biModal IT is underway?
<--- Score

60. What is the biModal IT's sustainability risk?
<--- Score

61. How do you develop, update and customize a roadmap to implement bimodal IT and adaptive sourcing?
<--- Score

62. To what extent does management recognize biModal IT as a tool to increase the results?
<--- Score

63. What do you want to improve?
<--- Score

64. What is the team's contingency plan for potential problems occurring in implementation?
<--- Score

65. Is there a cost/benefit analysis of optimal solution(s)?
<--- Score

66. What is the magnitude of the improvements?
<--- Score

67. How does the team improve its work?
<--- Score

68. Why improve in the first place?
<--- Score

69. How do you keep improving biModal IT?
<--- Score

70. In the past few months, what is the smallest change you have made that has had the biggest positive result? What was it about that small change that produced the large return?
<--- Score

71. How does the solution remove the key sources of issues discovered in the analyze phase?
<--- Score

72. Are possible solutions generated and tested?
<--- Score

73. Do you have any/correct application documentation?
<--- Score

74. Were any criteria developed to assist the team in testing and evaluating potential solutions?
<--- Score

75. How will you know when its improved?
<--- Score

76. Who will be responsible for documenting the biModal IT requirements in detail?
<--- Score

77. Describe the design of the pilot and what tests were conducted, if any?

<--- Score

78. What lessons, if any, from a pilot were incorporated into the design of the full-scale solution?
<--- Score

79. Who will be using the results of the measurement activities?
<--- Score

80. What to do with the results or outcomes of measurements?
<--- Score

81. There are often different developers at different times working on code; How much redundant code or technical debt is there in the code?
<--- Score

82. Can you identify any significant risks or exposures to biModal IT third- parties (vendors, service providers, alliance partners etc) that concern you?
<--- Score

83. Is pilot data collected and analyzed?
<--- Score

84. For estimation problems, how do you develop an estimation statement?
<--- Score

85. How do you link measurement and risk?
<--- Score

86. How do you improve productivity?

<--- Score

87. Who controls key decisions that will be made?
<--- Score

88. Is the solution technically practical?
<--- Score

89. How do you improve your likelihood of success ?
<--- Score

90. Is the scope clearly documented?
<--- Score

91. Are risk triggers captured?
<--- Score

92. Is a contingency plan established?
<--- Score

93. Will the controls trigger any other risks?
<--- Score

94. Is a solution implementation plan established, including schedule/work breakdown structure, resources, risk management plan, cost/budget, and control plan?
<--- Score

95. Can the solution be designed and implemented within an acceptable time period?
<--- Score

96. Are the best solutions selected?
<--- Score

97. Is there a small-scale pilot for proposed improvement(s)? What conclusions were drawn from the outcomes of a pilot?
<--- Score

98. Is the measure of success for biModal IT understandable to a variety of people?
<--- Score

99. What are your current levels and trends in key measures or indicators of workforce and leader development?
<--- Score

100. If you could go back in time five years, what decision would you make differently? What is your best guess as to what decision you're making today you might regret five years from now?
<--- Score

101. Do you have to redevelop my existing applications to be Mode 2 or use cloud?
<--- Score

102. How do you measure risk?
<--- Score

Add up total points for this section:
_ _ _ _ _ = Total points for this section

Divided by: _ _ _ _ _ _ (number of statements answered) = _ _ _ _ _ _
Average score for this section

Transfer your score to the biModal IT Index at the beginning of the Self-

Assessment.

CRITERION #6: CONTROL:

INTENT: Implement the practical solution. Maintain the performance and correct possible complications.

In my belief, the answer to this question is clearly defined:

5 Strongly Agree

4 Agree

3 Neutral

2 Disagree

1 Strongly Disagree

1. How will report readings be checked to effectively monitor performance?
<--- Score

2. Is reporting being used or needed?
<--- Score

3. Is knowledge gained on process shared and institutionalized?

<--- Score

4. Are documented procedures clear and easy to follow for the operators?
<--- Score

5. How likely is the current biModal IT plan to come in on schedule or on budget?
<--- Score

6. How do you select, collect, align, and integrate biModal IT data and information for tracking daily operations and overall organizational performance, including progress relative to strategic objectives and action plans?
<--- Score

7. How do you establish and deploy modified action plans if circumstances require a shift in plans and rapid execution of new plans?
<--- Score

8. To grow to such an extent that, soon, a significant portion of IT budgets will no longer be under the IT departments direct control. How are organisations to handle this inevitable change?
<--- Score

9. What key inputs and outputs are being measured on an ongoing basis?
<--- Score

10. What other areas of the organization might benefit from the biModal IT team's improvements, knowledge, and learning?
<--- Score

11. What are you attempting to measure/monitor?
<--- Score

12. What is the control/monitoring plan?
<--- Score

13. Is there a biModal IT Communication plan covering who needs to get what information when?
<--- Score

14. Who is the biModal IT process owner?
<--- Score

15. Will any special training be provided for results interpretation?
<--- Score

16. Is a response plan in place for when the input, process, or output measures indicate an 'out-of-control' condition?
<--- Score

17. Is there a documented and implemented monitoring plan?
<--- Score

18. What should you measure to verify efficiency gains?
<--- Score

19. Are controls in place and consistently applied?
<--- Score

20. Can support from partners be adjusted?
<--- Score

21. Do you monitor the biModal IT decisions made and fine tune them as they evolve?

<--- Score

22. Is there documentation that will support the successful operation of the improvement?

<--- Score

23. What do you measure to verify effectiveness gains?

<--- Score

24. Do you monitor the effectiveness of your biModal IT activities?

<--- Score

25. Is there a standardized process?

<--- Score

26. Who sets the biModal IT standards?

<--- Score

27. What quality tools were useful in the control phase?

<--- Score

28. Are pertinent alerts monitored, analyzed and distributed to appropriate personnel?

<--- Score

29. Which standard to adopt?

<--- Score

30. How will input, process, and output variables be checked to detect for sub-optimal conditions?

<--- Score

31. Can you adapt and adjust to changing biModal IT situations?
<--- Score

32. How might the organization capture best practices and lessons learned so as to leverage improvements across the business?
<--- Score

33. How do you plan on providing proper recognition and disclosure of supporting companies?
<--- Score

34. What should the next improvement project be that is related to biModal IT?
<--- Score

35. What other systems, operations, processes, and infrastructures (hiring practices, staffing, training, incentives/rewards, metrics/dashboards/scorecards, etc.) need updates, additions, changes, or deletions in order to facilitate knowledge transfer and improvements?
<--- Score

36. What are the known security controls?
<--- Score

37. Does a troubleshooting guide exist or is it needed?
<--- Score

38. How will new or emerging customer needs/ requirements be checked/communicated to orient the process toward meeting the new specifications

and continually reducing variation?
<--- Score

39. Who controls critical resources?
<--- Score

40. What do your reports reflect?
<--- Score

41. Who has control over resources?
<--- Score

42. How will the day-to-day responsibilities for monitoring and continual improvement be transferred from the improvement team to the process owner?
<--- Score

43. Where do ideas that reach policy makers and planners as proposals for biModal IT strengthening and reform actually originate?
<--- Score

44. Are there documented procedures?
<--- Score

45. How will you measure your QA plan's effectiveness?
<--- Score

46. Is there a transfer of ownership and knowledge to process owner and process team tasked with the responsibilities.
<--- Score

47. Is there a recommended audit plan for routine

surveillance inspections of biModal IT's gains?
<--- Score

48. Will your goals reflect your program budget?
<--- Score

49. Does job training on the documented procedures need to be part of the process team's education and training?
<--- Score

50. Has the improved process and its steps been standardized?
<--- Score

51. Are the planned controls in place?
<--- Score

52. What is the best design framework for biModal IT organization now that, in a post industrial-age if the top-down, command and control model is no longer relevant?
<--- Score

53. Does the response plan contain a definite closed loop continual improvement scheme (e.g., plan-do-check-act)?
<--- Score

54. How do controls support value?
<--- Score

55. Are suggested corrective/restorative actions indicated on the response plan for known causes to problems that might surface?
<--- Score

56. Is there a control plan in place for sustaining improvements (short and long-term)?
<--- Score

57. Who will be in control?
<--- Score

58. Does biModal IT appropriately measure and monitor risk?
<--- Score

59. Is a response plan established and deployed?
<--- Score

60. Will the team be available to assist members in planning investigations?
<--- Score

61. Are you measuring, monitoring and predicting biModal IT activities to optimize operations and profitability, and enhancing outcomes?
<--- Score

62. Do the biModal IT decisions you make today help people and the planet tomorrow?
<--- Score

63. What do you stand for--and what are you against?
<--- Score

64. How will the process owner and team be able to hold the gains?
<--- Score

65. What are the critical parameters to watch?

<--- Score

66. How will the process owner verify improvement in present and future sigma levels, process capabilities?
<--- Score

67. How do you maintain the appropriate security controls and governance in this continuous delivery and integration environment?
<--- Score

68. What is the recommended frequency of auditing?
<--- Score

69. What can you control?
<--- Score

70. What is your theory of human motivation, and how does your compensation plan fit with that view?
<--- Score

71. Implementation Planning: is a pilot needed to test the changes before a full roll out occurs?
<--- Score

72. What adjustments to the strategies are needed?
<--- Score

73. Does the biModal IT performance meet the customer's requirements?
<--- Score

74. How do your controls stack up?
<--- Score

75. Are operating procedures consistent?

<--- Score

76. How is change control managed?
<--- Score

77. Have new or revised work instructions resulted?
<--- Score

78. Act/Adjust: What Do you Need to Do Differently?
<--- Score

79. In the case of a biModal IT project, the criteria for the audit derive from implementation objectives. an audit of a biModal IT project involves assessing whether the recommendations outlined for implementation have been met. Can you track that any biModal IT project is implemented as planned, and is it working?
<--- Score

80. You may have created your quality measures at a time when you lacked resources, technology wasn't up to the required standard, or low service levels were the industry norm. Have those circumstances changed?
<--- Score

81. Are the planned controls working?
<--- Score

82. Is new knowledge gained imbedded in the response plan?
<--- Score

83. Are new process steps, standards, and documentation ingrained into normal operations?

<--- Score

84. How do senior leaders actions reflect a commitment to the organizations biModal IT values?
<--- Score

Add up total points for this section:
_ _ _ _ _ = Total points for this section

Divided by: _ _ _ _ _ _ (number of statements answered) = _ _ _ _ _ _
Average score for this section

Transfer your score to the biModal IT Index at the beginning of the Self-Assessment.

CRITERION #7: SUSTAIN:

INTENT: Retain the benefits.

In my belief, the answer to this question is clearly defined:

5 Strongly Agree

4 Agree

3 Neutral

2 Disagree

1 Strongly Disagree

1. Is your basic point _____ or _____?
<--- Score

2. Do you see more potential in people than they do in themselves?
<--- Score

3. What are your most important goals for the strategic biModal IT objectives?
<--- Score

4. What value do architects deliver?
<--- Score

5. Are the assumptions believable and achievable?
<--- Score

6. How do you get the best from your architects?
<--- Score

7. What are the barriers to increased biModal IT production?
<--- Score

8. What are the potential basics of biModal IT fraud?
<--- Score

9. What relationships among biModal IT trends do you perceive?
<--- Score

10. What have you done to protect your business from competitive encroachment?
<--- Score

11. Why not do biModal IT?
<--- Score

12. If you weren't already in this business, would you enter it today? And if not, what are you going to do about it?
<--- Score

13. What is your formula for success in biModal IT ?
<--- Score

14. What is the range of capabilities?

<--- Score

15. How can you negotiate biModal IT successfully with a stubborn boss, an irate client, or a deceitful coworker?
<--- Score

16. Where is architecture?
<--- Score

17. Do you have enough freaky customers in your portfolio pushing you to the limit day in and day out?
<--- Score

18. Political -is anyone trying to undermine this project?
<--- Score

19. How is this relevant today?
<--- Score

20. Have benefits been optimized with all key stakeholders?
<--- Score

21. Will there be any necessary staff changes (redundancies or new hires)?
<--- Score

22. Is a biModal IT team work effort in place?
<--- Score

23. To whom do you add value?
<--- Score

24. How will you motivate the stakeholders with the

least vested interest?
<--- Score

25. What goals did you miss?
<--- Score

26. What are internal and external biModal IT relations?
<--- Score

27. Can you do all this work?
<--- Score

28. Do you have past biModal IT successes?
<--- Score

29. Operational - will it work?
<--- Score

30. How much contingency will be available in the budget?
<--- Score

31. Whose voice (department, ethnic group, women, older workers, etc) might you have missed hearing from in your company, and how might you amplify this voice to create positive momentum for your business?
<--- Score

32. Are assumptions made in biModal IT stated explicitly?
<--- Score

33. Start small or big?
<--- Score

34. Who is responsible for ensuring appropriate resources (time, people and money) are allocated to biModal IT?
<--- Score

35. Who are the key stakeholders?
<--- Score

36. What information is critical to your organization that your executives are ignoring?
<--- Score

37. How can you become the company that would put you out of business?
<--- Score

38. How do you keep records, of what?
<--- Score

39. Should you buy vs build applications?
<--- Score

40. What are the new security challenges for managing bimodal IT?
<--- Score

41. How will you know that the biModal IT project has been successful?
<--- Score

42. What biModal IT modifications can you make work for you?
<--- Score

43. How do you provide a safe environment

-physically and emotionally?
<--- Score

44. Ask yourself: how would you do this work if you only had one staff member to do it?
<--- Score

45. Is biModal IT dependent on the successful delivery of a current project?
<--- Score

46. Were lessons learned captured and communicated?
<--- Score

47. In the past year, what have you done (or could you have done) to increase the accurate perception of your company/brand as ethical and honest?
<--- Score

48. What is something you believe that nearly no one agrees with you on?
<--- Score

49. What is the source of the strategies for biModal IT strengthening and reform?
<--- Score

50. How do you set biModal IT stretch targets and how do you get people to not only participate in setting these stretch targets but also that they strive to achieve these?
<--- Score

51. Which biModal IT goals are the most important?
<--- Score

52. What are specific biModal IT rules to follow?
<--- Score

53. What will be the consequences to the stakeholder (financial, reputation etc) if biModal IT does not go ahead or fails to deliver the objectives?
<--- Score

54. So how is mode 2 security different?
<--- Score

55. Is biModal IT realistic, or are you setting yourself up for failure?
<--- Score

56. Is there any reason to believe the opposite of my current belief?
<--- Score

57. Who do we want your customers to become?
<--- Score

58. How do you accomplish your long range biModal IT goals?
<--- Score

59. Marketing budgets are tighter, consumers are more skeptical, and social media has changed forever the way we talk about biModal IT. How do you gain traction?
<--- Score

60. Can you reduce spend without compromising speed to market as the portfolio evolves to an increasingly Agile-DevOps, Bimodal IT model?

<--- Score

61. How long will it take to change?
<--- Score

62. If no one would ever find out about your accomplishments, how would you lead differently?
<--- Score

63. Is the impact that biModal IT has shown?
<--- Score

64. What new services of functionality will be implemented next with biModal IT ?
<--- Score

65. Think of your biModal IT project, what are the main functions?
<--- Score

66. How much does biModal IT help?
<--- Score

67. What is your competitive advantage?
<--- Score

68. What trophy do you want on your mantle?
<--- Score

69. Is the code well commented?
<--- Score

70. What happens at your organization when people fail?
<--- Score

71. Why is biModal IT important for you now?
<--- Score

72. Do you have an implicit bias for capital investments over people investments?
<--- Score

73. Who, on the executive team or the board, has spoken to a customer recently?
<--- Score

74. Have new benefits been realized?
<--- Score

75. Surfing a digital wave, or drowning?
<--- Score

76. What trouble can you get into?
<--- Score

77. How can you incorporate support to ensure safe and effective use of biModal IT into the services that you provide?
<--- Score

78. How do you know if you are successful?
<--- Score

79. What is an unauthorized commitment?
<--- Score

80. If you were responsible for initiating and implementing major changes in your organization, what steps might you take to ensure acceptance of those changes?
<--- Score

81. How can you best use all of your knowledge repositories to enhance learning and sharing?
<--- Score

82. Do you say no to customers for no reason?
<--- Score

83. Can the schedule be done in the given time?
<--- Score

84. Is it necessary to implement bimodal IT and adaptive sourcing?
<--- Score

85. What management system can you use to leverage the biModal IT experience, ideas, and concerns of the people closest to the work to be done?
<--- Score

86. Who do you want your customers to become?
<--- Score

87. Do you have the right people on the bus?
<--- Score

88. Where can you break convention?
<--- Score

89. How important is biModal IT to the user organizations mission?
<--- Score

90. How do you ensure that implementations of biModal IT products are done in a way that ensures

safety?
<--- Score

91. What does your signature ensure?
<--- Score

92. Is there a work around that you can use?
<--- Score

93. Why should people listen to you?
<--- Score

94. What counts that you are not counting?
<--- Score

95. What did you miss in the interview for the worst hire you ever made?
<--- Score

96. What does Digital & IoT mean for your organization?
<--- Score

97. What do we do when new problems arise?
<--- Score

98. What are the essentials of internal biModal IT management?
<--- Score

99. What are the long-term biModal IT goals?
<--- Score

100. Who will be responsible for deciding whether biModal IT goes ahead or not after the initial investigations?

<--- Score

101. Are you maintaining a past–present–future perspective throughout the biModal IT discussion?
<--- Score

102. Who have you, as a company, historically been when you've been at your best?
<--- Score

103. How do you attract good architects?
<--- Score

104. What must you excel at?
<--- Score

105. How do you lead with biModal IT in mind?
<--- Score

106. How do you keep the momentum going?
<--- Score

107. Are the criteria for selecting recommendations stated?
<--- Score

108. Is it economical; do you have the time and money?
<--- Score

109. What are the gaps in your knowledge and experience?
<--- Score

110. If your customer were your grandmother, would you tell her to buy what you're selling?

<--- Score

111. If you got fired and a new hire took your place, what would she do different?
<--- Score

112. Did you do something great in Digital & IoT yet?
<--- Score

113. How is bimodal IT realized in practice?
<--- Score

114. What is the funding source for this project?
<--- Score

115. What should you stop doing?
<--- Score

116. Why DevSecOps and Agile?
<--- Score

117. Are you changing as fast as the world around you?
<--- Score

118. Do you have the right capabilities and capacities?
<--- Score

119. How likely is it that a customer would recommend your company to a friend or colleague?
<--- Score

120. Who will determine interim and final deadlines?
<--- Score

121. Are you satisfied with your current role? If not, what is missing from it?
<--- Score

122. How does biModal IT integrate with other business initiatives?
<--- Score

123. How do you engage the workforce, in addition to satisfying them?
<--- Score

124. What happens if you do not have enough funding?
<--- Score

125. Why should you adopt a biModal IT framework?
<--- Score

126. How do you deal with biModal IT changes?
<--- Score

127. What kind of crime could a potential new hire have committed that would not only not disqualify him/her from being hired by your organization, but would actually indicate that he/she might be a particularly good fit?
<--- Score

128. What biModal IT skills are most important?
<--- Score

129. Who uses your product in ways you never expected?
<--- Score

130. Why will customers want to buy your organizations products/services?
<--- Score

131. What projects are going on in the organization today, and what resources are those projects using from the resource pools?
<--- Score

132. What are the challenges?
<--- Score

133. What are strategies for increasing support and reducing opposition?
<--- Score

134. In a project to restructure biModal IT outcomes, which stakeholders would you involve?
<--- Score

135. Are new benefits received and understood?
<--- Score

136. When information truly is ubiquitous, when reach and connectivity are completely global, when computing resources are infinite, and when a whole new set of impossibilities are not only possible, but happening, what will that do to your business?
<--- Score

137. What stupid rule would you most like to kill?
<--- Score

138. How are you positioned?
<--- Score

139. Do you think you know, or do you know you know ?
<--- Score

140. What unique value proposition (UVP) do you offer?
<--- Score

141. Are you / should you be revolutionary or evolutionary?
<--- Score

142. Why is it important to have senior management support for a biModal IT project?
<--- Score

143. Do you feel that more should be done in the biModal IT area?
<--- Score

144. What happens when a new employee joins the organization?
<--- Score

145. What is it like to work for you?
<--- Score

146. Why would anyone want to be an architect in your enterprise?
<--- Score

147. Are you relevant? Will you be relevant five years from now? Ten?
<--- Score

148. If you do not follow, then how to lead?

<--- Score

149. Who is responsible for biModal IT?
<--- Score

150. What is meant by bimodal distribution?
<--- Score

151. What are the short and long-term biModal IT goals?
<--- Score

152. Would you rather sell to knowledgeable and informed customers or to uninformed customers?
<--- Score

153. How do you decide how much to remunerate an employee?
<--- Score

154. What is your question? Why?
<--- Score

155. If your company went out of business tomorrow, would anyone who doesn't get a paycheck here care?
<--- Score

156. What role does communication play in the success or failure of a biModal IT project?
<--- Score

157. Who do you think the world wants your organization to be?
<--- Score

158. Who are your customers?

<--- Score

159. How do you determine the key elements that affect biModal IT workforce satisfaction, how are these elements determined for different workforce groups and segments?
<--- Score

160. Can you break it down?
<--- Score

161. How do you make it meaningful in connecting biModal IT with what users do day-to-day?
<--- Score

162. Which functions and people interact with the supplier and or customer?
<--- Score

163. Has implementation been effective in reaching specified objectives so far?
<--- Score

164. Do you know what you are doing? And who do you call if you don't?
<--- Score

165. What threat is biModal IT addressing?
<--- Score

166. How do you stay inspired?
<--- Score

167. How can you become more high-tech but still be high touch?
<--- Score

168. How much redundant code or technical debt is there in the code?
<--- Score

169. If there were zero limitations, what would you do differently?
<--- Score

170. What one word do you want to own in the minds of your customers, employees, and partners?
<--- Score

171. How do you govern and fulfill your societal responsibilities?
<--- Score

172. What are the usability implications of biModal IT actions?
<--- Score

173. Who will manage the integration of tools?
<--- Score

174. Rigidity of your current asset base – what's the value of current assets on your balance sheet that may not be fit for purpose in the future and will inhibit growth?
<--- Score

175. Will it be accepted by users?
<--- Score

176. What was the last experiment you ran?
<--- Score

177. Can you maintain your growth without detracting from the factors that have contributed to your success?
<--- Score

178. What are the top 3 things at the forefront of your biModal IT agendas for the next 3 years?
<--- Score

179. When and under what conditions does your organization consider a bimodal IT design?
<--- Score

180. How do you listen to customers to obtain actionable information?
<--- Score

181. What current systems have to be understood and/or changed?
<--- Score

182. Do you think biModal IT accomplishes the goals you expect it to accomplish?
<--- Score

183. What is a feasible sequencing of reform initiatives over time?
<--- Score

184. How is alignment affected by bimodal IT?
<--- Score

185. What would you recommend your friend do if he/she were facing this dilemma?
<--- Score

186. What is creating tension between IT and business leaders?

<--- Score

187. At what moment would you think; Will I get fired?

<--- Score

188. What is the purpose of biModal IT in relation to the mission?

<--- Score

189. Do biModal IT rules make a reasonable demand on a users capabilities?

<--- Score

190. Why do and why don't your customers like your organization?

<--- Score

191. What are current biModal IT paradigms?

<--- Score

192. How do you go about securing biModal IT?

<--- Score

193. Is maximizing biModal IT protection the same as minimizing biModal IT loss?

<--- Score

194. What you are going to do to affect the numbers?

<--- Score

195. Are there any activities that you can take off your to do list?

<--- Score

196. If you had to leave your organization for a year and the only communication you could have with employees/colleagues was a single paragraph, what would you write?
<--- Score

197. What are your personal philosophies regarding biModal IT and how do they influence your work?
<--- Score

198. Who is responsible for errors?
<--- Score

199. Are there any disadvantages to implementing biModal IT? There might be some that are less obvious?
<--- Score

200. Who is on the team?
<--- Score

201. Who else should you help?
<--- Score

202. How do you cross-sell and up-sell your biModal IT success?
<--- Score

203. What are you challenging?
<--- Score

204. How will you insure seamless interoperability of biModal IT moving forward?
<--- Score

205. How do you proactively clarify deliverables and

biModal IT quality expectations?
<--- Score

206. Which individuals, teams or departments will be involved in biModal IT?
<--- Score

207. Scalability of resources – can your existing network and infrastructure react to a change in demand?
<--- Score

208. Are all key stakeholders present at all Structured Walkthroughs?
<--- Score

209. How do you foster the skills, knowledge, talents, attributes, and characteristics you want to have?
<--- Score

210. Who are four people whose careers you have enhanced?
<--- Score

211. What is the kind of project structure that would be appropriate for your biModal IT project, should it be formal and complex, or can it be less formal and relatively simple?
<--- Score

212. In retrospect, of the projects that you pulled the plug on, what percent do you wish had been allowed to keep going, and what percent do you wish had ended earlier?
<--- Score

213. What business benefits will biModal IT goals deliver if achieved?
<--- Score

214. What would have to be true for the option on the table to be the best possible choice?
<--- Score

215. How is implementation research currently incorporated into each of your goals?
<--- Score

216. What are the success criteria that will indicate that biModal IT objectives have been met and the benefits delivered?
<--- Score

217. Instead of going to current contacts for new ideas, what if you reconnected with dormant contacts--the people you used to know? If you were going reactivate a dormant tie, who would it be?
<--- Score

218. How do you retain good architects?
<--- Score

219. What have been your experiences in defining long range biModal IT goals?
<--- Score

220. Are you making progress, and are you making progress as biModal IT leaders?
<--- Score

221. Whom among your colleagues do you trust, and for what?

<--- Score

222. How are you doing compared to your industry?
<--- Score

223. What are the rules and assumptions your industry operates under? What if the opposite were true?
<--- Score

224. What are the key enablers to make this biModal IT move?
<--- Score

225. What is the recommended frequency of auditing?
<--- Score

226. Why are microservices important to Bi-modal IT?
<--- Score

227. What is the estimated value of the project?
<--- Score

228. How do you create buy-in?
<--- Score

229. Is the biModal IT organization completing tasks effectively and efficiently?
<--- Score

230. How do customers see your organization?
<--- Score

231. Who will provide the final approval of biModal IT deliverables?
<--- Score

232. Which models, tools and techniques are necessary?
<--- Score

233. Are you paying enough attention to the partners your company depends on to succeed?
<--- Score

234. How do you assess the biModal IT pitfalls that are inherent in implementing it?
<--- Score

235. Are your responses positive or negative?
<--- Score

236. How will you ensure you get what you expected?
<--- Score

237. What is the craziest thing you can do?
<--- Score

238. How do you progress to enterprise bimodal and what traps should you avoid?
<--- Score

239. What are the business goals biModal IT is aiming to achieve?
<--- Score

240. How do you transition from the baseline to the target?
<--- Score

241. How do you track customer value, profitability or financial return, organizational success, and

sustainability?
<--- Score

242. What are you trying to prove to yourself, and how might it be hijacking your life and business success?
<--- Score

243. How is business-IT alignment affected by a bimodal IT organization?
<--- Score

244. Did your employees make progress today?
<--- Score

245. What is effective biModal IT?
<--- Score

Add up total points for this section:
_ _ _ _ _ = Total points for this section

Divided by: _ _ _ _ _ _ (number of statements answered) = _ _ _ _ _ _
Average score for this section

Transfer your score to the biModal IT Index at the beginning of the Self-Assessment.

biModal IT and Managing Projects, Criteria for Project Managers:

1.0 Initiating Process Group: biModal IT

1. Do you understand all business (operational), technical, resource and vendor risks associated with the biModal IT project?

2. In which biModal IT project management process group is the detailed biModal IT project budget created?

3. Are you certain deliverables are properly completed and meet quality standards?

4. At which stage, in a typical biModal IT project do stake holders have maximum influence?

5. Were resources available as planned?

6. What will you do?

7. Do you know the roles & responsibilities required for this biModal IT project?

8. What communication items need improvement?

9. Specific - is the objective clear in terms of what, how, when, and where the situation will be changed?

10. Did the biModal IT project team have the right skills?

11. What will be the pressing issues of tomorrow?

12. The process to Manage Stakeholders is part of

which process group?

13. For technology biModal IT projects only: Are all production support stakeholders (Business unit, technical support, & user) prepared for implementation with appropriate contingency plans?

14. Measurable - are the targets measurable?

15. What do they need to know about the biModal IT project?

16. Were decisions made in a timely manner?

17. Did you use a contractor or vendor?

18. If the risk event occurs, what will you do?

19. How will it affect me?

20. When will the biModal IT project be done?

1.1 Project Charter: biModal IT

21. Customer: who are you doing the biModal IT project for?

22. When will this occur?

23. What are the known stakeholder requirements?

24. Who manages integration?

25. Will this replace an existing product?

26. What is the business need?

27. biModal IT project deliverables: what is the biModal IT project going to produce?

28. How high should you set your goals?

29. Review the general mission What system will be affected by the improvement efforts?

30. Who is the biModal IT project Manager?

31. Why use a biModal IT project charter?

32. How are biModal IT projects different from operations?

33. Assumptions: what factors, for planning purposes, are you considering to be true?

34. Environmental stewardship and sustainability

considerations: what is the process that will be used to ensure compliance with the environmental stewardship policy?

35. Why do you need to manage scope?

36. biModal IT project objective statement: what must the biModal IT project do?

37. How much?

38. What is in it for you?

39. What are the deliverables?

40. What ideas do you have for initial tests of change (PDSA cycles)?

1.2 Stakeholder Register: biModal IT

41. What are the major biModal IT project milestones requiring communications or providing communications opportunities?

42. How should employers make voices heard?

43. Who wants to talk about Security?

44. What & Why?

45. Who is managing stakeholder engagement?

46. How big is the gap?

47. What opportunities exist to provide communications?

48. What is the power of the stakeholder?

49. Is your organization ready for change?

50. How will reports be created?

51. How much influence do they have on the biModal IT project?

52. Who are the stakeholders?

1.3 Stakeholder Analysis Matrix: biModal IT

53. Accreditations, qualifications, certifications?

54. Management cover, succession?

55. What do people from other organizations see as your strengths?

56. Gaps in capabilities?

57. Guiding question: who shall you involve in the making of the stakeholder map?

58. How will the stakeholder directly benefit from the biModal IT project and how will this affect the stakeholders motivation?

59. Why do you need to manage biModal IT project Risk?

60. It developments?

61. Industry or lifestyle trends?

62. How do customers express needs?

63. Sustainable financial backing?

64. Partnerships, agencies, distribution?

65. Which resources are required?

66. Who influences whom?

67. Does your organization have bad debt or cash-flow problems?

68. How do rules, behaviors affect stakes?

69. What are the mechanisms of public and social accountability, and how can they be made better?

70. Why do you care?

71. Who will be affected by the work?

72. Lack of competitive strength?

2.0 Planning Process Group: biModal IT

73. Are there efficient coordination mechanisms to avoid overloading the counterparts, participating stakeholders?

74. How will you know you did it?

75. Why do it biModal IT projects fail?

76. To what extent are the visions and actions of the partners consistent or divergent with regard to the program?

77. Are the follow-up indicators relevant and do they meet the quality needed to measure the outputs and outcomes of the biModal IT project?

78. How well defined and documented are the biModal IT project management processes you chose to use?

79. To what extent is the program helping to influence your organizations policy framework?

80. How well did the chosen processes fit the needs of the biModal IT project?

81. Just how important is your work to the overall success of the biModal IT project?

82. Is the pace of implementing the products of the

program ensuring the completeness of the results of the biModal IT project?

83. How many days can task X be late in starting without affecting the biModal IT project completion date?

84. How will you do it?

85. Do the partners have sufficient financial capacity to keep up the benefits produced by the programme?

86. How are the principles of aid effectiveness (ownership, alignment, management for development results and mutual responsibility) being applied in the biModal IT project?

87. In what way has the program contributed towards the issue culture and development included on the public agenda?

88. On which process should team members spend the most time?

89. In what way has the biModal IT project come up with innovative measures for problem-solving?

90. Did the program design/ implementation strategy adequately address the planning stage necessary to set up structures, hire staff etc.?

91. What types of differentiated effects are resulting from the biModal IT project and to what extent?

92. Why is it important to determine activity sequencing on biModal IT projects?

2.1 Project Management Plan: biModal IT

93. What are the assumptions?

94. What is risk management?

95. Will you add a schedule and diagram?

96. When is the biModal IT project management plan created?

97. What would you do differently?

98. How well are you able to manage your risk?

99. What data/reports/tools/etc. do program managers need?

100. If the biModal IT project is complex or scope is specialized, do you have appropriate and/or qualified staff available to perform the tasks?

101. What is biModal IT project scope management?

102. How can you best help your organization to develop consistent practices in biModal IT project management planning stages?

103. What would you do differently what did not work?

104. Are calculations and results of analyzes

essentially correct?

105. What is the justification?

106. What data/reports/tools/etc. do your PMs need?

107. What are the constraints?

108. How do you manage time?

109. Why Change?

110. Did the planning effort collaborate to develop solutions that integrate expertise, policies, programs, and biModal IT projects across entities?

111. What worked well?

2.2 Scope Management Plan: biModal IT

112. Has the selected plan been formulated using cost effectiveness and incremental analysis techniques?

113. Has the biModal IT project manager been identified?

114. Knowing the health of the biModal IT project – What is the status?

115. Are there any windfall benefits that would accrue to the biModal IT project sponsor or other parties?

116. What do you need to do to accomplish the goal or goals?

117. For which criterion is it tolerable not to meet the original parameters?

118. Have the scope, objectives, costs, benefits and impacts been communicated to all involved and/or impacted stakeholders and work groups?

119. Without-plan conditions?

120. Will the biModal IT project deliverables become accepted in writing?

121. Has the schedule been baselined?

122. Has stakeholder analysis been conducted,

assessing influence on the biModal IT project and authority levels?

123. Are risk oriented checklists used during risk identification?

124. Is stakeholder involvement adequate?

125. Are the biModal IT project plans updated on a frequent basis?

126. How much money have you spent?

127. Are biModal IT project team members committed fulltime?

128. Are the schedule estimates reasonable given the biModal IT project?

129. Have the personnel with the necessary skills and competence been identified and has agreement for participation in the biModal IT project been reached with the appropriate management?

130. Has appropriate allowance been made for the effect of the learning curve on all personnel joining the biModal IT project who do not have the required prior industry, functional & technical expertise?

131. Are trade-offs between accepting the risk and mitigating the risk identified?

2.3 Requirements Management Plan: biModal IT

132. Has the requirements team been instructed in the Change Control process?

133. Who will perform the analysis?

134. Will the contractors involved take full responsibility?

135. How will requirements be managed?

136. What are you counting on?

137. Does the biModal IT project have a Change Control process?

138. Do you have price sheets and a methodology for determining the total proposal cost?

139. Who will initially review the biModal IT project work or products to ensure it meets the applicable acceptance criteria?

140. To see if a requirement statement is sufficiently well-defined, read it from the developers perspective. Mentally add the phrase, call me when youre done to the end of the requirement and see if that makes you nervous. In other words, would you need additional clarification from the author to understand the requirement well enough to design and implement it?

141. Will you perform a Requirements Risk assessment and develop a plan to deal with risks?

142. Describe the process for rejecting the biModal IT project requirements. Who has the authority to reject biModal IT project requirements?

143. Who will do the reporting and to whom will reports be delivered?

144. What are you trying to do?

145. Will you document changes to requirements?

146. How knowledgeable is the team in the proposed application area?

147. What information regarding the biModal IT project requirements will be reported?

148. Is there formal agreement on who has authority to approve a change in requirements?

149. Will the biModal IT project requirements become approved in writing?

150. If it exists, where is it housed?

151. Who is responsible for monitoring and tracking the biModal IT project requirements?

2.4 Requirements Documentation: biModal IT

152. How linear / iterative is your Requirements Gathering process (or will it be)?

153. What will be the integration problems?

154. Are there any requirements conflicts?

155. Who is involved?

156. Basic work/business process; high-level, what is being touched?

157. Have the benefits identified with the system being identified clearly?

158. How will requirements be documented and who signs off on them?

159. Where do system and software requirements come from, what are sources?

160. How do you know when a Requirement is accurate enough?

161. What facilities must be supported by the system?

162. Does the system provide the functions which best support the customers needs?

163. Where are business rules being captured?

164. Are there legal issues?

165. Does your organization restrict technical alternatives?

166. What if the system wasn t implemented?

167. How can you document system requirements?

168. Are all functions required by the customer included?

169. What happens when requirements are wrong?

170. Do your constraints stand?

171. Is the origin of the requirement clearly stated?

2.5 Requirements Traceability Matrix: biModal IT

172. How do you manage scope?

173. Do you have a clear understanding of all subcontracts in place?

174. Is there a requirements traceability process in place?

175. How will it affect the stakeholders personally in their career?

176. What are the chronologies, contingencies, consequences, criteria?

177. Describe the process for approving requirements so they can be added to the traceability matrix and biModal IT project work can be performed. Will the biModal IT project requirements become approved in writing?

178. Will you use a Requirements Traceability Matrix?

179. Why do you manage scope?

180. What is the WBS?

181. How small is small enough?

182. What percentage of biModal IT projects are producing traceability matrices between

requirements and other work products?

183. Why use a WBS?

2.6 Project Scope Statement: biModal IT

184. Will there be a Change Control Process in place?

185. What process would you recommend for creating the biModal IT project scope statement?

186. Relevant - ask yourself can you get there; why are you doing this biModal IT project?

187. If there is an independent oversight contractor, have they signed off on the biModal IT project Plan?

188. If the scope changes, what will the impact be to your biModal IT project in terms of duration, cost, quality, or any other important areas of the biModal IT project?

189. Were potential customers involved early in the planning process?

190. Are there backup strategies for key members of the biModal IT project?

191. What are the major deliverables of the biModal IT project?

192. Is there a process (test plans, inspections, reviews) defined for verifying outputs for each task?

193. Will this process be communicated to the customer and biModal IT project team?

194. Identify how your team and you will create the biModal IT project scope statement and the work breakdown structure (WBS). Document how you will create the biModal IT project scope statement and WBS, and make sure you answer the following questions: In defining biModal IT project scope and the WBS, will you and your biModal IT project team be using methods defined by your organization, methods defined by the biModal IT project management office (PMO), or other methods?

195. Is the biModal IT project manager qualified and experienced in biModal IT project management?

196. How often will scope changes be reviewed?

197. Is there a Change Management Board?

198. Does the scope statement still need some clarity?

199. If there are vendors, have they signed off on the biModal IT project Plan?

200. Was planning completed before the biModal IT project was initiated?

201. Has the format for tracking and monitoring schedules and costs been defined?

2.7 Assumption and Constraint Log: biModal IT

202. What to do at recovery?

203. Is the current scope of the biModal IT project substantially different than that originally defined in the approved biModal IT project plan?

204. When can log be discarded?

205. Is there adequate stakeholder participation for the vetting of requirements definition, changes and management?

206. What would you gain if you spent time working to improve this process?

207. What strengths do you have?

208. Security analysis has access to information that is sanitized?

209. How are new requirements or changes to requirements identified?

210. Are there processes defining how software will be developed including development methods, overall timeline for development, software product standards, and traceability?

211. Have all stakeholders been identified?

212. Have biModal IT project management standards and procedures been established and documented?

213. Are requirements management tracking tools and procedures in place?

214. What if failure during recovery?

215. Contradictory information between document sections?

216. What other teams / processes would be impacted by changes to the current process, and how?

217. Have all involved stakeholders and work groups committed to the biModal IT project?

218. Have you eliminated all duplicative tasks or manual efforts, where appropriate?

219. If appropriate, is the deliverable content consistent with current biModal IT project documents and in compliance with the Document Management Plan?

220. What threats might prevent you from getting there?

221. Is the process working, and people are not executing in compliance of the process?

2.8 Work Breakdown Structure: biModal IT

222. How will you and your biModal IT project team define the biModal IT projects scope and work breakdown structure?

223. How big is a work-package?

224. Is it a change in scope?

225. Why would you develop a Work Breakdown Structure?

226. How much detail?

227. When do you stop?

228. What has to be done?

229. Is it still viable?

230. Why is it useful?

231. When would you develop a Work Breakdown Structure?

232. What is the probability that the biModal IT project duration will exceed xx weeks?

233. Do you need another level?

234. What is the probability of completing the

biModal IT project in less that xx days?

235. How many levels?

236. Where does it take place?

237. Who has to do it?

238. Can you make it?

239. How far down?

240. Is the work breakdown structure (wbs) defined and is the scope of the biModal IT project clear with assigned deliverable owners?

241. When does it have to be done?

2.9 WBS Dictionary: biModal IT

242. Are work packages reasonably short in time duration or do they have adequate objective indicators/milestones to minimize subjectivity of the in process work evaluation?

243. Is work properly classified as measured effort, LOE, or apportioned effort and appropriately separated?

244. Budgets assigned to control accounts?

245. Identify potential or actual budget-based and time-based schedule variances?

246. Do procedures specify under what circumstances replanning of open work packages may occur, and the methods to be followed?

247. Are retroactive changes to BCWS and BCWP prohibited except for correction of errors or for normal accounting adjustments?

248. Evaluate the performance of operating organizations?

249. Are procedures established to prevent changes to the contract budget base other than the already stated authorized by contractual action?

250. Are procedures in existence that control replanning of unopened work packages, and are corresponding procedures adhered to?

251. Software specification, development, integration, and testing, licenses ?

252. Intermediate schedules, as required, which provide a logical sequence from the master schedule to the control account level?

253. Does the contractors system provide for accurate cost accumulation and assignment to control accounts in a manner consistent with the budgets using recognized acceptable costing techniques?

254. Identify potential or actual overruns and underruns?

255. Are budgets or values assigned to work packages and planning packages in terms of dollars, hours, or other measurable units?

256. Are records maintained to show how management reserves are used?

257. Are your organizations and items of cost assigned to each pool identified?

258. Do work packages consist of discrete tasks which are adequately described?

259. Does the sum of all work package budgets plus planning packages within control accounts equal the budgets assigned to the already stated control accounts?

260. Changes in the direct base to which overhead costs are allocated?

261. Does the contractors system include procedures for measuring performance of the lowest level organization responsible for the control account?

2.10 Schedule Management Plan: biModal IT

262. Are the processes for status updates and maintenance defined?

263. Are meeting objectives identified for each meeting?

264. Are the constraints or deadlines associated with the task accurate?

265. Identify the amount of schedule variation that triggers a warning. What happens if a warning is triggered?

266. Is there general agreement & acceptance of the current status and progress of the biModal IT project?

267. Are biModal IT project team members involved in detailed estimating and scheduling?

268. Are the processes for schedule assessment and analysis defined?

269. Are corrective actions and variances reported?

270. Are all payments made according to the contract(s)?

271. Is pert / critical path or equivalent methodology being used?

272. Were biModal IT project team members involved in the development of activity & task decomposition?

273. Are right task and resource calendars used in the IMS?

274. Is a process defined for baseline approval and control?

275. Have all involved biModal IT project stakeholders and work groups committed to the biModal IT project?

276. Is the schedule vertically and horizontally traceable?

277. Are assumptions being identified, recorded, analyzed, qualified and closed?

278. Is there a formal set of procedures supporting Issues Management?

279. Define units of measurement for each resource. For example, are you referencing gallons or liters?

280. Are mitigation strategies identified?

281. Have all team members been part of identifying risks?

2.11 Activity List: biModal IT

282. What went right?

283. How will it be performed?

284. Where will it be performed?

285. What went well?

286. How can the biModal IT project be displayed graphically to better visualize the activities?

287. In what sequence?

288. What is your organizations history in doing similar activities?

289. For other activities, how much delay can be tolerated?

290. Is there anything planned that does not need to be here?

291. What will be performed?

292. Who will perform the work?

293. What did not go as well?

294. How detailed should a biModal IT project get?

295. What is the LF and LS for each activity?

296. What is the total time required to complete the biModal IT project if no delays occur?

297. What is the probability the biModal IT project can be completed in xx weeks?

298. When will the work be performed?

299. How difficult will it be to do specific activities on this biModal IT project?

300. When do the individual activities need to start and finish?

301. The wbs is developed as part of a joint planning session. and how do you know that youhave done this right?

2.12 Activity Attributes: biModal IT

302. Activity: what is Missing?

303. What is the general pattern here?

304. Can you re-assign any activities to another resource to resolve an over-allocation?

305. Would you consider either of corresponding activities an outlier?

306. Have you identified the Activity Leveling Priority code value on each activity?

307. Do you feel very comfortable with your prediction?

308. How many days do you need to complete the work scope with a limit of X number of resources?

309. How many resources do you need to complete the work scope within a limit of X number of days?

310. Activity: what is In the Bag?

311. Is there a trend during the year?

312. What conclusions/generalizations can you draw from this?

313. How much activity detail is required?

314. Time for overtime?

315. How difficult will it be to complete specific activities on this biModal IT project?

316. Does your organization of the data change its meaning?

317. What activity do you think you should spend the most time on?

318. Why?

319. Were there other ways you could have organized the data to achieve similar results?

320. Which method produces the more accurate cost assignment?

2.13 Milestone List: biModal IT

321. Milestone pages should display the UserID of the person who added the milestone. Does a report or query exist that provides this audit information?

322. It is to be a narrative text providing the crucial aspects of your biModal IT project proposal answering what, who, how, when and where?

323. Describe the industry you are in and the market growth opportunities. What is the market for your technology, product or service?

324. Information and research?

325. Insurmountable weaknesses?

326. Which path is the critical path?

327. Vital contracts and partners?

328. Legislative effects?

329. Political effects?

330. Calculate how long can activity be delayed?

331. Own known vulnerabilities?

332. What is the market for your technology, product or service?

333. What specific improvements did you make to the

biModal IT project proposal since the previous time?

334. How late can the activity finish?

335. Loss of key staff?

336. Marketing - reach, distribution, awareness?

337. How difficult will it be to do specific activities on this biModal IT project?

338. Describe your organizations strengths and core competencies. What factors will make your organization succeed?

2.14 Network Diagram: biModal IT

339. What activities must follow this activity?

340. What is the probability of completing the biModal IT project in less that xx days?

341. What activities must occur simultaneously with this activity?

342. How difficult will it be to do specific activities on this biModal IT project?

343. Review the logical flow of the network diagram. Take a look at which activities you have first and then sequence the activities. Do they make sense?

344. Where do you schedule uncertainty time?

345. Are you on time?

346. If x is long, what would be the completion time if you break x into two parallel parts of y weeks and z weeks?

347. How confident can you be in your milestone dates and the delivery date?

348. What must be completed before an activity can be started?

349. What can be done concurrently?

350. What controls the start and finish of a job?

351. Why must you schedule milestones, such as reviews, throughout the biModal IT project?

352. What is the completion time?

353. Planning: who, how long, what to do?

354. What are the tools?

355. Are the gantt chart and/or network diagram updated periodically and used to assess the overall biModal IT project timetable?

356. If a current contract exists, can you provide the vendor name, contract start, and contract expiration date?

357. Can you calculate the confidence level?

358. What are the Key Success Factors?

2.15 Activity Resource Requirements: biModal IT

359. Why do you do that?

360. Do you use tools like decomposition and rolling-wave planning to produce the activity list and other outputs?

361. Organizational Applicability?

362. Anything else?

363. How do you handle petty cash?

364. Other support in specific areas?

365. What are constraints that you might find during the Human Resource Planning process?

366. Are there unresolved issues that need to be addressed?

367. What is the Work Plan Standard?

368. Which logical relationship does the PDM use most often?

369. When does monitoring begin?

370. How many signatures do you require on a check and does this match what is in your policy and procedures?

2.16 Resource Breakdown Structure: biModal IT

371. What is each stakeholders desired outcome for the biModal IT project?

372. Are the required resources available?

373. The list could probably go on, but, the thing that you would most like to know is, How long & How much?

374. Any changes from stakeholders?

375. What is the number one predictor of a groups productivity?

376. How difficult will it be to do specific activities on this biModal IT project?

377. Is predictive resource analysis being done?

378. What went wrong?

379. Who is allowed to perform which functions?

380. Who delivers the information?

381. Why is this important?

382. Which resources should be in the resource pool?

383. What is the primary purpose of the human

resource plan?

384. Which resource planning tool provides information on resource responsibility and accountability?

385. What defines a successful biModal IT project?

386. Why do you do it?

2.17 Activity Duration Estimates: biModal IT

387. Are risks monitored to determine if an event has occurred or if the mitigation was successful?

388. What are the typical challenges biModal IT project teams face during each of the five process groups?

389. Are biModal IT project activities decomposed into manageable components to ensure expected management control?

390. What does it mean to take a systems view of a biModal IT project?

391. What is pmp certification, and why do you think the number of people earning it has grown so much in the past ten years?

392. Are biModal IT project costs tracked in the general ledger?

393. Do checklists exist that list frequently performed activities?

394. Write a oneto two-page paper describing your dream team for this biModal IT project. What type of people would you want on your team?

395. Does a process exist to identify individuals authorized to make certain decisions?

396. Describe a biModal IT project that suffered from scope creep. Could it have been avoided?

397. Which would be the NEXT thing for the biModal IT project manager to do?

398. How can organizations use a weighted decision matrix to evaluate proposals as part of source selection?

399. Are updates on work results collected and used as inputs to the performance reporting process?

400. Why is it important to determine activity sequencing on biModal IT projects?

401. Are contractor costs, schedule and technical performance monitored throughout the biModal IT project?

402. What are the largest companies that provide information technology outsourcing services?

403. biModal IT project manager has received activity duration estimates from his team. Which does one need in order to complete schedule development?

404. Who has the PRIMARY responsibility to solve this problem?

405. Are many products available?

406. biModal IT project has three critical paths. Which BEST describes how this affects the biModal IT project?

2.18 Duration Estimating Worksheet: biModal IT

407. What is your role?

408. What is an Average biModal IT project?

409. What info is needed?

410. What questions do you have?

411. Is this operation cost effective?

412. How can the biModal IT project be displayed graphically to better visualize the activities?

413. What utility impacts are there?

414. Value pocket identification & quantification what are value pockets?

415. Does the biModal IT project provide innovative ways for stakeholders to overcome obstacles or deliver better outcomes?

416. What is next?

417. Why estimate time and cost?

418. Small or large biModal IT project?

419. When does your organization expect to be able to complete it?

420. What work will be included in the biModal IT project?

421. Define the work as completely as possible. What work will be included in the biModal IT project?

422. Is the biModal IT project responsive to community need?

423. When, then?

424. How should ongoing costs be monitored to try to keep the biModal IT project within budget?

2.19 Project Schedule: biModal IT

425. Have all biModal IT project delays been adequately accounted for, communicated to all stakeholders and adjustments made in overall biModal IT project schedule?

426. How do you manage biModal IT project Risk?

427. What documents, if any, will the subcontractor provide (eg biModal IT project schedule, quality plan etc)?

428. What is the most mis-scheduled part of process?

429. Why do you think schedule issues often cause the most conflicts on biModal IT projects?

430. What does that mean?

431. Should you have a test for each code module?

432. What is risk?

433. What is biModal IT project management?

434. Are the original biModal IT project schedule and budget realistic?

435. Is the biModal IT project schedule available for all biModal IT project team members to review?

436. Meet requirements?

437. Should you include sub-activities?

438. Is infrastructure setup part of your biModal IT project?

439. To what degree is do you feel the entire team was committed to the biModal IT project schedule?

440. Are key risk mitigation strategies added to the biModal IT project schedule?

441. Was the biModal IT project schedule reviewed by all stakeholders and formally accepted?

442. How can slack be negative?

443. Are all remaining durations correct?

2.20 Cost Management Plan: biModal IT

444. Are the appropriate IT resources adequate to meet planned commitments?

445. Owner, contractor, and subcontractors?

446. Are biModal IT project contact logs kept up to date?

447. Were biModal IT project team members involved in detailed estimating and scheduling?

448. Has a quality assurance plan been developed for the biModal IT project?

449. Contracting method – what contracting method is to be used for the contracts?

450. Outside experts?

451. How difficult will it be to do specific tasks on the biModal IT project?

452. Similar biModal IT projects?

453. Is the steering committee active in biModal IT project oversight?

454. Is a payment system in place with proper reviews and approvals?

455. If you sold 10x widgets on a day, what would the affect on costs be?

456. Is there a formal set of procedures supporting Stakeholder Management?

457. What is the work breakdown structure for the biModal IT project?

458. Is quality monitored from the perspective of the customers needs and expectations?

459. Forecasts – how will the time and resources needed to complete the biModal IT project be forecast?

460. Are written status reports provided on a designated frequent basis?

461. Are tasks tracked by hours?

2.21 Activity Cost Estimates: biModal IT

462. Vac -variance at completion, how much over/ under budget do you expect to be?

463. Padding is bad and contingencies are good. what is the difference?

464. How do you fund change orders?

465. What defines a successful biModal IT project?

466. What is the activity recast of the budget?

467. What areas were overlooked on this biModal IT project?

468. What is the activity inventory?

469. What is the estimators estimating history?

470. Does the activity serve a common type of customer?

471. Will you need to provide essential services information about activities?

472. Was the consultant knowledgeable about the program?

473. How do you treat administrative costs in the activity inventory?

474. Can you change your activities?

475. What were things that you did very well and want to do the same again on the next biModal IT project?

476. How do you allocate indirect costs to activities?

477. One way to define activities is to consider how organization employees describe jobs to families and friends. You basically want to know, What do you do?

478. Who determines the quality and expertise of contractors?

479. What were things that you did well, and could improve, and how?

480. When do you enter into PPM?

481. Review – what are some common errors in activities to avoid?

2.22 Cost Estimating Worksheet: biModal IT

482. What costs are to be estimated?

483. How will the results be shared and to whom?

484. Identify the timeframe necessary to monitor progress and collect data to determine how the selected measure has changed?

485. Ask: are others positioned to know, are others credible, and will others cooperate?

486. Who is best positioned to know and assist in identifying corresponding factors?

487. What is the estimated labor cost today based upon this information?

488. Does the biModal IT project provide innovative ways for stakeholders to overcome obstacles or deliver better outcomes?

489. What happens to any remaining funds not used?

490. What additional biModal IT project(s) could be initiated as a result of this biModal IT project?

491. What can be included?

492. Is it feasible to establish a control group arrangement?

493. What is the purpose of estimating?

494. Will the biModal IT project collaborate with the local community and leverage resources?

495. Can a trend be established from historical performance data on the selected measure and are the criteria for using trend analysis or forecasting methods met?

496. What will others want?

497. Is the biModal IT project responsive to community need?

2.23 Cost Baseline: biModal IT

498. Escalation criteria met?

499. Has the actual cost of the biModal IT project (or biModal IT project phase) been tallied and compared to the approved budget?

500. Does it impact schedule, cost, quality?

501. Has operations management formally accepted responsibility for operating and maintaining the product(s) or service(s) delivered by the biModal IT project?

502. Verify business objectives. Are others appropriate, and well-articulated?

503. Are there contingencies or conditions related to the acceptance?

504. Are you asking management for something as a result of this update?

505. Are procedures defined by which the cost baseline may be changed?

506. How will cost estimates be used?

507. Has the documentation relating to operation and maintenance of the product(s) or service(s) been delivered to, and accepted by, operations management?

508. How difficult will it be to do specific tasks on the biModal IT project?

509. What is cost and biModal IT project cost management?

510. Who will use corresponding metrics ?

511. Does a process exist for establishing a cost baseline to measure biModal IT project performance?

512. What deliverables come first?

513. On budget?

514. Will the biModal IT project fail if the change request is not executed?

515. Where do changes come from?

516. Is request in line with priorities?

2.24 Quality Management Plan: biModal IT

517. Modifications to the requirements?

518. Who is responsible for approving the qapp?

519. How will you know that a change is actually an improvement?

520. Have all involved stakeholders and work groups committed to the biModal IT project?

521. Was trending evident between audits?

522. What process do you use to minimize errors, defects, and rework?

523. Are qmps good forever?

524. What are your organizations key processes (product, service, business, and support)?

525. How long do you retain data?

526. How do senior leaders create an environment that encourages learning and innovation?

527. Is a component/condition present?

528. How does your organization recruit, hire, and retain new employees?

529. Was trending evident between reviews?

530. How do you measure?

531. Are there standards for code development?

532. How do you decide what information to record?

533. When reporting to different audiences, do you vary the form or type of report?

534. With the five whys method, the team considers why the issue being explored occurred. do others then take that initial answer and ask why?

535. How are corresponding standards measured?

536. Were there any deficiencies / issues identified in the prior years self-assessment?

2.25 Quality Metrics: biModal IT

537. What makes a visualization memorable?

538. When is the security analysis testing complete?

539. Are documents on hand to provide explanations of privacy and confidentiality?

540. Were quality attributes reported?

541. How should customers provide input?

542. Do the operators focus on determining; is there anything you need to worry about?

543. What method of measurement do you use?

544. Is quality culture a competitive advantage?

545. Is a risk containment plan in place?

546. The metrics–what is being considered?

547. When will the Final Guidance will be issued?

548. If the defect rate during testing is substantially higher than that of the previous release (or a similar product), then ask: Did you plan for and actually improve testing effectiveness?

549. Has it met internal or external standards?

550. Filter visualizations of interest?

551. Which are the right metrics to use?

552. Where is quality now?

553. How do you calculate corresponding metrics?

554. Who is willing to lead?

555. Where did complaints, returns and warranty claims come from?

2.26 Process Improvement Plan: biModal IT

556. What is quality and how will you ensure it?

557. Have the frequency of collection and the points in the process where measurements will be made been determined?

558. The motive is determined by asking, Why do you want to achieve this goal?

559. What is the test-cycle concept?

560. Why do you want to achieve the goal?

561. Are you meeting the quality standards?

562. Where are you now?

563. Has a process guide to collect the data been developed?

564. Everyone agrees on what process improvement is, right?

565. Has the time line required to move measurement results from the points of collection to databases or users been established?

566. Are you following the quality standards?

567. To elicit goal statements, do you ask a question

such as, What do you want to achieve?

568. Does explicit definition of the measures exist?

569. Where do you focus?

570. What lessons have you learned so far?

571. Are there forms and procedures to collect and record the data?

572. What is the return on investment?

573. Where do you want to be?

574. How do you manage quality?

575. Management commitment at all levels?

2.27 Responsibility Assignment Matrix: biModal IT

576. Actual cost of work performed?

577. Who is the biModal IT project Manager?

578. No rs: if a task has no one listed as responsible, who is getting the job done?

579. Does the accounting system provide a basis for auditing records of direct costs chargeable to the contract?

580. Most people let you know when others re too busy, and are others really too busy?

581. The anticipated business volume?

582. Does the contractor use objective results, design reviews, and tests to trace schedule?

583. Incurrence of actual indirect costs in excess of budgets, by element of expense?

584. Evaluate the impact of schedule changes, work around, etc?

585. Are overhead cost budgets established for each organization which has authority to incur overhead costs?

586. Is data disseminated to the contractors

management timely, accurate, and usable?

587. Are the overhead pools formally and adequately identified?

588. The already stated responsible for the establishment of budgets and assignment of resources for overhead performance?

589. Will too many Signing-off responsibilities delay the completion of the activity/deliverable?

590. What materials and procurements needed?

591. Where does all this information come from?

592. Can the contractor substantiate work package and planning package budgets?

2.28 Roles and Responsibilities: biModal IT

593. Are your policies supportive of a culture of quality data?

594. Are governance roles and responsibilities documented?

595. Influence: what areas of organizational decision making are you able to influence when you do not have authority to make the final decision?

596. Once the responsibilities are defined for the biModal IT project, have the deliverables, roles and responsibilities been clearly communicated to every participant?

597. Who is responsible for each task?

598. What should you do now to prepare for your career 5+ years from now?

599. What areas would you highlight for changes or improvements?

600. Does the team have access to and ability to use data analysis tools?

601. Is there a training program in place for stakeholders covering expectations, roles and responsibilities and any addition knowledge others need to be good stakeholders?

602. Is feedback clearly communicated and non-judgmental?

603. What should you highlight for improvement?

604. Implementation of actions: Who are the responsible units?

605. Concern: where are you limited or have no authority, where you can not influence?

606. Where are you most strong as a supervisor?

607. What should you do now to ensure that you are meeting all expectations of your current position?

608. What should you do now to prepare yourself for a promotion, increased responsibilities or a different job?

609. Required skills, knowledge, experience?

610. Attainable / achievable: the goal is attainable; can you actually accomplish the goal?

611. Key conclusions and recommendations: Are conclusions and recommendations relevant and acceptable?

2.29 Human Resource Management Plan: biModal IT

612. Are risk triggers captured?

613. Are target dates established for each milestone deliverable?

614. Where is your organization headed?

615. Is your organization heading towards expansion, outsourcing of certain talents or making cut-backs to save money?

616. What areas does the group agree are the biggest success on the biModal IT project?

617. Is documentation created for communication with the suppliers and Vendors?

618. Are decisions captured in a decisions log?

619. List roles. what commitments have been made?

620. Do you have the reasons why the changes to your organizational systems and capabilities are required?

621. Has a capability assessment been conducted?

622. Has a resource management plan been created?

623. Were biModal IT project team members involved

in the development of activity & task decomposition?

624. Are procurement deliverables arriving on time and to specification?

625. Are adequate resources provided for the quality assurance function?

626. Have biModal IT project management standards and procedures been identified / established and documented?

627. Is it possible to track all classes of biModal IT project work (e.g. scheduled, un-scheduled, defect repair, etc.)?

628. Is there a set of procedures to capture, analyze and act on quality metrics?

2.30 Communications Management Plan: biModal IT

629. Are the stakeholders getting the information others need, are others consulted, are concerns addressed?

630. What communications method?

631. Why do you manage communications?

632. Are stakeholders internal or external?

633. How did the term stakeholder originate?

634. Who needs to know and how much?

635. What steps can you take for a positive relationship?

636. What to learn?

637. Who did you turn to if you had questions?

638. Where do team members get information?

639. How much time does it take to do it?

640. Do you ask; can you recommend others for you to talk with about this initiative?

641. Will messages be directly related to the release strategy or phases of the biModal IT project?

642. Do you feel more overwhelmed by stakeholders?

643. Are there potential barriers between the team and the stakeholder?

644. Are you constantly rushing from meeting to meeting?

645. Who is involved as you identify stakeholders?

646. What are the interrelationships?

647. Who will use or be affected by the result of a biModal IT project?

648. How is this initiative related to other portfolios, programs, or biModal IT projects?

2.31 Risk Management Plan: biModal IT

649. Are people attending meetings and doing work?

650. Is security a central objective?

651. What things are likely to change?

652. Does the biModal IT project have the authority and ability to avoid the risk?

653. What is the likelihood that your organization would accept responsibility for the risk?

654. Are requirements fully understood by the software engineering team and customers?

655. Maximize short-term return on investment?

656. Technology risk: is the biModal IT project technically feasible?

657. Are certain activities taking a long time to complete?

658. How is risk identification performed?

659. Could others have been better mitigated?

660. How risk averse are you?

661. Is there additional information that would make

you more confident about your analysis?

662. How is risk monitoring performed?

663. How much risk protection can you afford?

664. What risks are tracked?

665. What are the chances the event will occur?

666. Has something like this been done before?

667. Are the reports useful and easy to read?

2.32 Risk Register: biModal IT

668. What are your key risks/show istoppers and what is being done to manage them?

669. How are risks graded?

670. What are the main aims, objectives of the policy, strategy, or service and the intended outcomes?

671. How often will the Risk Management Plan and Risk Register be formally reviewed, and by whom?

672. Can the likelihood and impact of failing to achieve corresponding recommendations and action plans be assessed?

673. Do you require further engagement?

674. What is a Risk?

675. Are implemented controls working as others should?

676. Recovery actions - planned actions taken once a risk has occurred to allow you to move on. What should you do after?

677. Market risk -will the new service or product be useful to your organization or marketable to others?

678. What has changed since the last period?

679. Assume the risk event or situation happens, what

would the impact be?

680. What should you do when?

681. What would the impact to the biModal IT project objectives be should the risk arise?

682. How is a Community Risk Register created?

683. Is further information required before making a decision?

684. Amongst the action plans and recommendations that you have to introduce are there some that could stop or delay the overall program?

685. Which key risks have ineffective responses or outstanding improvement actions?

686. When will it happen?

687. Preventative actions - planned actions to reduce the likelihood a risk will occur and/or reduce the seriousness should it occur. What should you do now?

2.33 Probability and Impact Assessment: biModal IT

688. What are the current demands of the customer?

689. What will be the likely political environment during the life of the biModal IT project?

690. What significant shift will occur in governmental policies, laws, and regulations pertaining to specific industries?

691. Mitigation -how can you avoid the risk?

692. What is the experience (performance, attitude, business ethics, etc.) in the past with contractors?

693. How will economic events and trends likely affect the biModal IT project?

694. How much risk do others need to take?

695. What is the likelihood?

696. To what extent is the chosen technology maturing?

697. Will there be an increase in the political conservatism?

698. What can you do about it?

699. Does the customer understand the software

process?

700. Are some people working on multiple biModal IT projects?

701. Do you train all developers in the process?

702. Do you have a consistent repeatable process that is actually used?

703. Have customers been involved fully in the definition of requirements?

704. Can it be enlarged by drawing people from other areas of your organization?

705. Does the biModal IT project team have experience with the technology to be implemented?

706. What will be the likely political situation during the life of the biModal IT project?

2.34 Probability and Impact Matrix: biModal IT

707. What are the uncertainties associated with the technology selected for the biModal IT project?

708. Are biModal IT project requirements stable?

709. Do requirements demand the use of new analysis, design, or testing methods?

710. Which should be probably done NEXT?

711. What are the preparations required for facing difficulties?

712. Are there alternative opinions/solutions/ processes you should explore?

713. What will be the environmental impact of the biModal IT project?

714. Are formal technical reviews part of this process?

715. What action would you take to the identified risks in the biModal IT project?

716. What would be the effect of slippage?

717. How will the consumption pattern change?

718. Is biModal IT project scope stable?

719. How would you define a risk?

720. Can it be changed quickly?

721. While preparing your risk responses, you identify additional risks. What should you do?

722. How carefully have the potential competitors been identified?

723. What are the chances the risk events will occur?

2.35 Risk Data Sheet: biModal IT

724. Whom do you serve (customers)?

725. What do you know?

726. What are you weak at and therefore need to do better?

727. Has a sensitivity analysis been carried out?

728. What if client refuses?

729. How reliable is the data source?

730. Who has a vested interest in how you perform as your organization (our stakeholders)?

731. What are you trying to achieve (Objectives)?

732. Type of risk identified?

733. What can you do?

734. Do effective diagnostic tests exist?

735. What are the main threats to your existence?

736. What actions can be taken to eliminate or remove risk?

737. Has the most cost-effective solution been chosen?

738. What was measured?

739. What is the chance that it will happen?

740. How do you handle product safely?

741. Risk of what?

742. What do people affected think about the need for, and practicality of preventive measures?

743. How can hazards be reduced?

2.36 Procurement Management Plan: biModal IT

744. Is the schedule updated on a periodic basis?

745. Are post milestone biModal IT project reviews (PMPR) conducted with your organization at least once a year?

746. Does the schedule include biModal IT project management time and change request analysis time?

747. Have all documents been archived in a biModal IT project repository for each release?

748. Is there a requirements change management processes in place?

749. Does the biModal IT project have a formal biModal IT project Charter?

750. Is the communication plan being followed?

751. How will multiple providers be managed?

752. Have the key functions and capabilities been defined and assigned to each release or iteration?

753. Are the quality tools and methods identified in the Quality Plan appropriate to the biModal IT project?

754. Does the resource management plan include a

personnel development plan?

755. Has the biModal IT project manager been identified?

756. In which phase of the Acquisition Process Cycle does source qualifications reside?

757. Do biModal IT project managers participating in the biModal IT project know the biModal IT projects true status first hand?

758. What are you trying to accomplish?

759. Have lessons learned been conducted after each biModal IT project release?

760. Are the schedule estimates reasonable given the biModal IT project?

761. Have all necessary approvals been obtained?

762. Are the payment terms being followed?

2.37 Source Selection Criteria: biModal IT

763. What are the limitations on pre-competitive range communications?

764. When should debriefings be held and how should they be scheduled?

765. Is a letter of commitment from each proposed team member and key subcontractor included?

766. When is it appropriate to issue a DRFP?

767. Who is entitled to a debriefing?

768. Do you want to have them collaborate at subfactor level?

769. Are types/quantities of material, facilities appropriate?

770. How do you manage procurement?

771. Which contract type places the most risk on the seller?

772. Why promote competition?

773. How much weight should be placed on past performance information?

774. What are the guiding principles for developing

an evaluation report?

775. When and what information can be considered with offerors regarding past performance?

776. What are the special considerations for preaward debriefings?

777. If the costs are normalized, please account for how the normalization is conducted. Is a cost realism analysis used?

778. What evidence should be provided regarding proposal evaluations?

779. How should the solicitation aspects regarding past performance be structured?

780. How should comments received in response to a RFP be handled?

781. Are responses to considerations adequate?

782. Are they compliant with all technical requirements?

2.38 Stakeholder Management Plan: biModal IT

783. Are communication systems currently in place appropriate?

784. Are communication systems proposed compatible with staff skills and experience?

785. Do any protocols apply for records management?

786. Is the process working, and are people executing in compliance of the process?

787. Are all key components of a Quality Assurance Plan present?

788. Who is responsible for the post implementation review process?

789. What are the advantages and disadvantages of using external contracted resources?

790. Are estimating assumptions and constraints captured?

791. What are reporting requirements?

792. Does the biModal IT project have a formal biModal IT project Charter?

793. What proven methodologies and standards will be used to ensure that materials, products, processes

and services are fit for purpose?

794. Have biModal IT project management standards and procedures been identified / established and documented?

795. Is there an onboarding process in place?

796. Have external dependencies been captured in the schedule?

797. How are you doing/what can be done better?

798. Who is gathering information?

799. Are changes in scope (deliverable commitments) agreed to by all affected groups & individuals?

800. Have adequate resources been provided by management to ensure biModal IT project success?

801. Are biModal IT project team members committed fulltime?

2.39 Change Management Plan: biModal IT

802. What does a resilient organization look like?

803. What goal(s) do you hope to accomplish?

804. Will all field readiness criteria have been practically met prior to training roll-out?

805. Who is the target audience of the piece of information?

806. Has this been negotiated with the customer and sponsor?

807. Is there an adequate supply of people for the new roles?

808. Who should be involved in developing a change management strategy?

809. What policies and procedures need to be changed?

810. What risks may occur upfront, during implementation and after implementation?

811. What work practices will be affected?

812. Is there a support model for this application and are the details available for distribution?

813. What are the training strategies?

814. Has the training co-ordinator been provided with the training details and put in place the necessary arrangements?

815. Has an information & communications plan been developed?

816. What is the negative impact of communicating too soon or too late?

817. Which relationships will change?

818. What would be an estimate of the total cost for the activities required to carry out the change initiative?

819. Where will the funds come from?

820. How badly can information be misinterpreted?

3.0 Executing Process Group: biModal IT

821. Why should biModal IT project managers strive to make jobs look easy?

822. Is the program supported by national and/or local organizations?

823. Is the schedule for the set products being met?

824. What are the challenges biModal IT project teams face?

825. What is the difference between using brainstorming and the Delphi technique for risk identification?

826. What type of information goes in the quality assurance plan?

827. Will new hardware or software be required for servers or client machines?

828. How do you measure difficulty?

829. What are some crucial elements of a good biModal IT project plan?

830. Who are the biModal IT project stakeholders?

831. How does a biModal IT project life cycle differ from a product life cycle?

832. When is the appropriate time to bring the scorecard to Board meetings?

833. Do biModal IT project managers understand your organizational context for biModal IT projects?

834. Does the biModal IT project team have the right skills?

835. How well did the team follow the chosen processes?

836. How can software assist in biModal IT project communications?

837. How will you avoid scope creep?

838. What are the main processes included in biModal IT project quality management?

839. Have operating capacities been created and/or reinforced in partners?

840. Contingency planning. if a risk event occurs, what will you do?

3.1 Team Member Status Report: biModal IT

841. Does your organization have the means (staff, money, contract, etc.) to produce or to acquire the product, good, or service?

842. How will resource planning be done?

843. Does every department have to have a biModal IT project Manager on staff?

844. When a teams productivity and success depend on collaboration and the efficient flow of information, what generally fails them?

845. Does the product, good, or service already exist within your organization?

846. Are your organizations biModal IT projects more successful over time?

847. What specific interest groups do you have in place?

848. How much risk is involved?

849. The problem with Reward & Recognition Programs is that the truly deserving people all too often get left out. How can you make it practical?

850. How does this product, good, or service meet the needs of the biModal IT project and your organization

as a whole?

851. How can you make it practical?

852. Will the staff do training or is that done by a third party?

853. Why is it to be done?

854. Are the products of your organizations biModal IT projects meeting customers objectives?

855. What is to be done?

856. Are the attitudes of staff regarding biModal IT project work improving?

857. Do you have an Enterprise biModal IT project Management Office (EPMO)?

858. Is there evidence that staff is taking a more professional approach toward management of your organizations biModal IT projects?

859. How it is to be done?

3.2 Change Request: biModal IT

860. Who is responsible to authorize changes?

861. Are you implementing itil processes?

862. Are there requirements attributes that are strongly related to the occurrence of defects and failures?

863. Who will perform the change?

864. When to submit a change request?

865. What is the relationship between requirements attributes and reliability?

866. Who is responsible for the implementation and monitoring of all measures?

867. How to get changes (code) out in a timely manner?

868. What is the purpose of change control?

869. What are the duties of the change control team?

870. Will the change use memory to the extent that other functions will be not have sufficient memory to operate effectively?

871. What is a Change Request Form?

872. Since there are no change requests in your

biModal IT project at this point, what must you have before you begin?

873. How does your organization control changes before and after software is released to a customer?

874. Will there be a change request form in use?

875. Are there requirements attributes that are strongly related to the complexity and size?

876. What has an inspector to inspect and to check?

877. What is the change request log?

878. Can you answer what happened, who did it, when did it happen, and what else will be affected?

3.3 Change Log: biModal IT

879. Will the biModal IT project fail if the change request is not executed?

880. Is the change request open, closed or pending?

881. Do the described changes impact on the integrity or security of the system?

882. When was the request submitted?

883. Is the requested change request a result of changes in other biModal IT project(s)?

884. How does this relate to the standards developed for specific business processes?

885. Is the change request within biModal IT project scope?

886. When was the request approved?

887. Does the suggested change request represent a desired enhancement to the products functionality?

888. How does this change affect the timeline of the schedule?

889. Should a more thorough impact analysis be conducted?

890. How does this change affect scope?

891. Does the suggested change request seem to represent a necessary enhancement to the product?

892. Is the change backward compatible without limitations?

893. Is this a mandatory replacement?

894. Is the submitted change a new change or a modification of a previously approved change?

895. Who initiated the change request?

3.4 Decision Log: biModal IT

896. How effective is maintaining the log at facilitating organizational learning?

897. What was the rationale for the decision?

898. Is everything working as expected?

899. How do you define success?

900. What alternatives/risks were considered?

901. With whom was the decision shared or considered?

902. Adversarial environment. is your opponent open to a non-traditional workflow, or will it likely challenge anything you do?

903. Behaviors; what are guidelines that the team has identified that will assist them with getting the most out of team meetings?

904. Linked to original objective?

905. What is the average size of your matters in an applicable measurement?

906. What eDiscovery problem or issue did your organization set out to fix or make better?

907. Is your opponent open to a non-traditional workflow, or will it likely challenge anything you do?

908. Does anything need to be adjusted?

909. Meeting purpose; why does this team meet?

910. At what point in time does loss become unacceptable?

911. How consolidated and comprehensive a story can you tell by capturing currently available incident data in a central location and through a log of key decisions during an incident?

912. What is your overall strategy for quality control / quality assurance procedures?

913. Decision-making process; how will the team make decisions?

914. How do you know when you are achieving it?

915. Who is the decisionmaker?

3.5 Quality Audit: biModal IT

916. How does your organization know that its promotions system is appropriately effective, constructive and fair?

917. Are goals well supported with strategies, operational plans, manuals and training?

918. How is the Strategic Plan (and other plans) reviewed and revised?

919. Can your organization demonstrate exactly how and why results were achieved?

920. How does your organization know that the research supervision provided to its staff is appropriately effective and constructive?

921. Do prior clients have a positive opinion of your organization?

922. What does an analysis of your organizations staff profile suggest in terms of its planning, and how is this being addressed?

923. How does your organization ensure that equipment is appropriately maintained and producing valid results?

924. Does the suppliers quality system have a written procedure for corrective action when a defect occurs?

925. How does your organization know that it

provides a safe and healthy environment?

926. How does your organization know that its general support services planning and management systems are appropriately effective and constructive?

927. How does your organization know that its Mission, Vision and Values Statements are appropriate and effectively guiding your organization?

928. How does your organization know that its system for managing intellectual property issues is appropriately effective, constructive and fair?

929. How well do you think your organization engages with the outside community?

930. How does your organization know that it is maintaining a conducive staff climate?

931. How does your organization know that its relationships with the community at large are appropriately effective and constructive?

932. What happens if your organization fails its Quality Audit?

933. Are multiple statements on the same issue consistent with each other?

934. What is the collective experience of the team to be assigned to an audit?

935. How does your organization know that its system for recruiting the best staff possible are appropriately effective and constructive?

3.6 Team Directory: biModal IT

936. Does a biModal IT project team directory list all resources assigned to the biModal IT project?

937. Process decisions: are there any statutory or regulatory issues relevant to the timely execution of work?

938. Who will be the stakeholders on your next biModal IT project?

939. Where will the product be used and/or delivered or built when appropriate?

940. How will you accomplish and manage the objectives?

941. How and in what format should information be presented?

942. Who is the Sponsor?

943. How do unidentified risks impact the outcome of the biModal IT project?

944. When does information need to be distributed?

945. Decisions: what could be done better to improve the quality of the constructed product?

946. How will the team handle changes?

947. Is construction on schedule?

948. Contract requirements complied with?

949. Process decisions: is work progressing on schedule and per contract requirements?

950. Decisions: is the most suitable form of contract being used?

951. What needs to be communicated?

952. Who are your stakeholders (customers, sponsors, end users, team members)?

953. Where should the information be distributed?

954. Process decisions: which organizational elements and which individuals will be assigned management functions?

955. Who will talk to the customer?

3.7 Team Operating Agreement: biModal IT

956. Are leadership responsibilities shared among team members (versus a single leader)?

957. Conflict resolution: how will disputes and other conflicts be mediated or resolved?

958. Do you upload presentation materials in advance and test the technology?

959. Do you determine the meeting length and time of day?

960. Do you post any action items, due dates, and responsibilities on the team website?

961. Do team members reside in more than two countries?

962. Do you begin with a question to engage everyone?

963. What administrative supports will be put in place to support the team and the teams supervisor?

964. What individual strengths does each team member bring to the group?

965. What is the number of cases currently teamed?

966. Did you prepare participants for the next

meeting?

967. What resources can be provided for the team in terms of equipment, space, time for training, protected time and space for meetings, and travel allowances?

968. Are team roles clearly defined and accepted?

969. What are some potential sources of conflict among team members?

970. Do team members need to frequently communicate as a full group to make timely decisions?

971. Have you established procedures that team members can follow to work effectively together, such as a team operating agreement?

972. Are there the right people on your team?

973. Why does your organization want to participate in teaming?

974. What is teaming?

3.8 Team Performance Assessment: biModal IT

975. Can familiarity breed backup?

976. To what degree do team members understand one anothers roles and skills?

977. To what degree can team members frequently and easily communicate with one another?

978. To what degree is the team cognizant of small wins to be celebrated along the way?

979. To what degree do team members feel that the purpose of the team is important, if not exciting?

980. To what degree do team members frequently explore the teams purpose and its implications?

981. How does biModal IT project termination impact biModal IT project team members?

982. Lack of method variance in self-reported affect and perceptions at work: Reality or artifact?

983. Do friends perform better than acquaintances?

984. How do you manage human resources?

985. What do you think is the most constructive thing that could be done now to resolve considerations and disputes about method variance?

986. To what degree do members articulate the goals beyond the team membership?

987. Which situations call for a more extreme type of adaptiveness in which team members actually re-define roles?

988. To what degree do the goals specify concrete team work products?

989. To what degree can team members vigorously define the teams purpose in considerations with others who are not part of the functioning team?

990. To what degree do members understand and articulate the same purpose without relying on ambiguous abstractions?

991. What is method variance?

992. To what degree are fresh input and perspectives systematically caught and added (for example, through information and analysis, new members, and senior sponsors)?

993. Can team performance be reliably measured in simulator and live exercises using the same assessment tool?

994. To what degree does the teams purpose contain themes that are particularly meaningful and memorable?

3.9 Team Member Performance Assessment: biModal IT

995. Does adaptive training work?

996. How do you use data to inform instruction and improve staff achievement?

997. What are the key duties or tasks of the Ratee?

998. To what extent did the evaluation influence the instructional path, such as with adaptive testing?

999. What are the staffs preferences for training on technology-based platforms?

1000. Is there reluctance to join a team?

1001. What changes do you need to make to align practices with beliefs?

1002. What innovations (if any) are developed to realize goals?

1003. How are training activities developed from a technical perspective?

1004. Can your organization rate by exception and assume that most employees are performing at an acceptable level?

1005. To what degree is there a sense that only the team can succeed?

1006. Has the appropriate access to relevant data and analysis capability been granted?

1007. What stakeholders must be involved in the development and oversight of the performance plan?

1008. To what degree can all members engage in open and interactive considerations?

1009. To what degree will new and supplemental skills be introduced as the need is recognized?

1010. How do you implement Cost Reduction?

1011. How should adaptive assessments be implemented?

1012. What is a general description of the processes under performance measurement and assessment?

1013. What are the basic principles and objectives of performance measurement and assessment?

3.10 Issue Log: biModal IT

1014. Do you often overlook a key stakeholder or stakeholder group?

1015. What is the stakeholders political influence?

1016. What is the impact on the risks?

1017. How is this initiative related to other portfolios, programs, or biModal IT projects?

1018. What would have to change?

1019. Why not more evaluators?

1020. What approaches to you feel are the best ones to use?

1021. Who reported the issue?

1022. Can you think of other people who might have concerns or interests?

1023. Are the stakeholders getting the information they need, are they consulted, are concerns addressed?

1024. Is access to the Issue Log controlled?

1025. What steps can you take for positive relationships?

1026. Do you prepare stakeholder engagement plans?

1027. Do you feel a register helps?

4.0 Monitoring and Controlling Process Group: biModal IT

1028. Is progress on outcomes due to your program?

1029. Did it work?

1030. How well did the chosen processes produce the expected results?

1031. Change, where should you look for problems?

1032. Did the biModal IT project team have enough people to execute the biModal IT project plan?

1033. How will staff learn how to use the deliverables?

1034. What were things that you need to improve?

1035. User: who wants the information and what are they interested in?

1036. Who needs to be engaged upfront to ensure use of results?

1037. What areas does the group agree are the biggest success on the biModal IT project?

1038. How well did the chosen processes fit the needs of the biModal IT project?

1039. Is there sufficient funding available for this?

1040. Purpose: toward what end is the evaluation being conducted?

1041. Key stakeholders to work with. How many potential communications channels exist on the biModal IT project?

1042. When will the biModal IT project be done?

1043. What factors are contributing to progress or delay in the achievement of products and results?

1044. Do the products created live up to the necessary quality?

4.1 Project Performance Report: biModal IT

1045. To what degree is there centralized control of information sharing?

1046. To what degree does the funding match the requirement?

1047. To what degree are the skill areas critical to team performance present?

1048. To what degree will the team ensure that all members equitably share the work essential to the success of the team?

1049. To what degree are the goals ambitious?

1050. To what degree does the teams approach to its work allow for modification and improvement over time?

1051. To what degree are the tasks requirements reflected in the flow and storage of information?

1052. To what degree do the relationships of the informal organization motivate taskrelevant behavior and facilitate task completion?

1053. To what degree do all members feel responsible for all agreed-upon measures?

1054. To what degree will the approach capitalize

on and enhance the skills of all team members in a manner that takes into consideration other demands on members of the team?

1055. What is the degree to which rules govern information exchange between individuals within your organization?

1056. To what degree are the demands of the task compatible with and converge with the relationships of the informal organization?

1057. To what degree does the teams work approach provide opportunity for members to engage in fact-based problem solving?

1058. To what degree will the team adopt a concrete, clearly understood, and agreed-upon approach that will result in achievement of the teams goals?

1059. To what degree is the information network consistent with the structure of the formal organization?

1060. To what degree does the teams work approach provide opportunity for members to engage in open interaction?

1061. To what degree are sub-teams possible or necessary?

4.2 Variance Analysis: biModal IT

1062. Are overhead costs budgets established on a basis consistent with the anticipated direct business base?

1063. Does the contractors system provide unit or lot costs when applicable?

1064. What is your organizations rationale for sharing expenses and services between business segments?

1065. Are indirect costs charged to the appropriate indirect pools and incurring organization?

1066. Does the contractors system identify work accomplishment against the schedule plan?

1067. What types of services and expense are shared between business segments?

1068. Is all contract work included in the CWBS?

1069. Contract line items and end items?

1070. Do the rates and prices remain constant throughout the year?

1071. Favorable or unfavorable variance?

1072. Are all authorized tasks assigned to identified organizational elements?

1073. Are the bases and rates for allocating costs from

each indirect pool consistently applied?

1074. How have the setting and use of standards changed over time?

1075. Can the relationship with problem customers be restructured so that there is a win-win situation?

1076. Who is generally responsible for monitoring and taking action on variances?

4.3 Earned Value Status: biModal IT

1077. How much is it going to cost by the finish?

1078. If earned value management (EVM) is so good in determining the true status of a biModal IT project and biModal IT project its completion, why is it that hardly any one uses it in information systems related biModal IT projects?

1079. Verification is a process of ensuring that the developed system satisfies the stakeholders agreements and specifications; Are you building the product right? What do you haverify?

1080. How does this compare with other biModal IT projects?

1081. Where is evidence-based earned value in your organization reported?

1082. Are you hitting your biModal IT projects targets?

1083. When is it going to finish?

1084. What is the unit of forecast value?

1085. Validation is a process of ensuring that the developed system will actually achieve the stakeholders desired outcomes; Are you building the right product? What do you validate?

1086. Earned value can be used in almost any biModal IT project situation and in almost any biModal IT project environment. it may be used on large biModal IT projects, medium sized biModal IT projects, tiny biModal IT projects (in cut-down form), complex and simple biModal IT projects and in any market sector. some people, of course, know all about earned value, they have used it for years - but perhaps not as effectively as they could have?

1087. Where are your problem areas?

4.4 Risk Audit: biModal IT

1088. Are auditors able to effectively apply more soft evidence found in the risk-assessment process with the results of more tangible audit evidence found through more substantive testing?

1089. What programmatic and Fiscal information is being collected and analyzed?

1090. Do all coaches/instructors/leaders have appropriate and current accreditation?

1091. Who is responsible for what?

1092. Do you meet the legislative requirements (for example PAYG, super contributions) for paid employees?

1093. Extending the consideration on the halo effect, to what extent are auditors able to build skepticism in evidence review?

1094. What can be measured?

1095. Have you reviewed your constitution within the last twelve months?

1096. Risks with biModal IT projects or new initiatives?

1097. Do you have proper induction processes for all new paid staff and volunteers who have a specific role and responsibility?

1098. What is happening in other jurisdictions? Could that happen here?

1099. Who audits the auditor?

1100. Is an annual audit required and conducted of your financial records?

1101. Are requirements fully understood by the team and customers?

1102. Is biModal IT project scope stable?

1103. Is there a clear procedure for reporting accidents/injuries?

1104. Does your organization have a process for meeting its ongoing taxation obligations?

1105. Does the customer have a solid idea of what is required?

1106. Have you considered the health and safety of everyone in your organization and do you meet work health and safety regulations?

4.5 Contractor Status Report: biModal IT

1107. If applicable; describe your standard schedule for new software version releases. Are new software version releases included in the standard maintenance plan?

1108. How long have you been using the services?

1109. What is the average response time for answering a support call?

1110. What was the final actual cost?

1111. What process manages the contracts?

1112. What are the minimum and optimal bandwidth requirements for the proposed soluiton?

1113. How is risk transferred?

1114. What was the overall budget or estimated cost?

1115. What was the budget or estimated cost for your organizations services?

1116. What was the actual budget or estimated cost for your organizations services?

1117. Are there contractual transfer concerns?

1118. Who can list a biModal IT project as organization

experience, your organization or a previous employee of your organization?

1119. Describe how often regular updates are made to the proposed solution. Are corresponding regular updates included in the standard maintenance plan?

1120. How does the proposed individual meet each requirement?

4.6 Formal Acceptance: biModal IT

1121. Was the biModal IT project goal achieved?

1122. What function(s) does it fill or meet?

1123. What can you do better next time?

1124. Have all comments been addressed?

1125. Do you buy pre-configured systems or build your own configuration?

1126. Does it do what biModal IT project team said it would?

1127. Do you buy-in installation services?

1128. Was the sponsor/customer satisfied?

1129. Was business value realized?

1130. Do you perform formal acceptance or burn-in tests?

1131. Was the biModal IT project work done on time, within budget, and according to specification?

1132. What lessons were learned about your biModal IT project management methodology?

1133. Was the biModal IT project managed well?

1134. How well did the team follow the methodology?

1135. Is formal acceptance of the biModal IT project product documented and distributed?

1136. Did the biModal IT project manager and team act in a professional and ethical manner?

1137. Was the client satisfied with the biModal IT project results?

1138. Does it do what client said it would?

1139. Who supplies data?

1140. Did the biModal IT project achieve its MOV?

5.0 Closing Process Group: biModal IT

1141. How well did the chosen processes fit the needs of the biModal IT project?

1142. Were sponsors and decision makers available when needed outside regularly scheduled meetings?

1143. What were things that you did very well and want to do the same again on the next biModal IT project?

1144. What were the desired outcomes?

1145. What is the risk of failure to your organization?

1146. Did the biModal IT project team have the right skills?

1147. Will the biModal IT project deliverable(s) replace a current asset or group of assets?

1148. How critical is the biModal IT project success to the success of your organization?

1149. What will you do to minimize the impact should a risk event occur?

1150. Can the lesson learned be replicated?

1151. Were the outcomes different from the already stated planned?

1152. What could have been improved?

1153. Were cost budgets met?

1154. Mitigate. what will you do to minimize the impact should a risk event occur?

5.1 Procurement Audit: biModal IT

1155. Is there no evidence that the expert has influenced the decisions taken by the public authority in his/her interest or in the interest of a specific contractor?

1156. Which contracts have been awarded for works, supply of products or provision of services?

1157. Was the expert likely to gain privileged knowledge from his activity which could be advantageous for him in a subsequent competition?

1158. Does the procurement function/unit understand costumer needs, supply markets and suppliers?

1159. Are behaviour modification applied to change procurement of goods and services if procurement is not functioning properly?

1160. Does the cash disbursement policy prohibit drawing checks to cash or bearer?

1161. Are risks managed to provide reasonable assurance regarding department procurement objectives?

1162. Does the procurement biModal IT project have a clear goal and does the goal meet the specified needs of the users?

1163. Does the department evaluate and benchmark

the performance of the procurement function/ unit against other comparable procurement functions/ units?

1164. Are there internal control systems in place to secure that laws and regulations are observed?

1165. Could the bidders assess the economic risks the successful bidder would be responsible for, thus limiting the inclusion of extra charges for risk?

1166. Are tenders who do not comply with the requirements specified in the request for tenders rejected?

1167. Are trial balances taken weekly for general ledgers for all funds?

1168. Are budget transfers within the general fund made for only the already stated items permitted by law and regulation?

1169. Are advantages and disadvantages of in-house production, outsourcing and Public Private Partnerships considered?

1170. Was all the key documentation given to the contracting authority?

1171. Are there policies regarding special approval for capital expenditures?

1172. Does the department have a procurement strategy and is it implemented?

1173. What are your ethical guidelines for public

procurement?

1174. Is a cost/benefit analysis, a cost/effectiveness or a financial analysis considering life-cycle costs performed and is the funding of the procurement guaranteed?

5.2 Contract Close-Out: biModal IT

1175. Has each contract been audited to verify acceptance and delivery?

1176. Was the contract complete without requiring numerous changes and revisions?

1177. Have all contracts been completed?

1178. How is the contracting office notified of the automatic contract close-out?

1179. Change in attitude or behavior?

1180. Parties: who is involved?

1181. Why Outsource?

1182. Have all contracts been closed?

1183. What happens to the recipient of services?

1184. Are the signers the authorized officials?

1185. Change in circumstances?

1186. Change in knowledge?

1187. Was the contract sufficiently clear so as not to result in numerous disputes and misunderstandings?

1188. Parties: Authorized?

1189. How does it work?

1190. Have all contract records been included in the biModal IT project archives?

1191. Have all acceptance criteria been met prior to final payment to contractors?

1192. Was the contract type appropriate?

1193. How/when used ?

1194. What is capture management?

5.3 Project or Phase Close-Out: biModal IT

1195. What are the informational communication needs for each stakeholder?

1196. Is there a clear cause and effect between the activity and the lesson learned?

1197. What is the information level of detail required for each stakeholder?

1198. Was the schedule met?

1199. What security considerations needed to be addressed during the procurement life cycle?

1200. Was the user/client satisfied with the end product?

1201. What is this stakeholder expecting?

1202. What advantages do the an individual interview have over a group meeting, and vice-versa?

1203. What were the actual outcomes?

1204. Complete yes or no?

1205. In addition to assessing whether the biModal IT project was successful, it is equally critical to analyze why it was or was not fully successful. Are you including this?

1206. What stakeholder group needs, expectations, and interests are being met by the biModal IT project?

1207. Who is responsible for award close-out?

1208. Did the delivered product meet the specified requirements and goals of the biModal IT project?

1209. Did the biModal IT project management methodology work?

1210. What information is each stakeholder group interested in?

1211. What are the mandatory communication needs for each stakeholder?

1212. What is a Risk Management Process?

5.4 Lessons Learned: biModal IT

1213. Whom to share Lessons Learned Information with?

1214. How effective was the acceptance management process?

1215. To what extent was the evolution of risks communicated?

1216. Was sufficient time allocated to review biModal IT project deliverables?

1217. What things mattered the most on this biModal IT project?

1218. How much flexibility is there in the funding (e.g., what authorities does the program manager have to change to the specifics of the funding within the overall funding ceiling)?

1219. Under what legal authority did your organization head and program manager direct your organization and biModal IT project?

1220. How well do you feel the executives supported this biModal IT project?

1221. What were the lessons learned on this biModal IT project?

1222. Was the control overhead justified?

1223. Did the biModal IT project improve the team members reputations, skills, personal development?

1224. How effective was biModal IT project Team member training?

1225. Was the biModal IT project significantly delayed/hampered by outside dependencies (outside to the biModal IT project, that is)?

1226. Was the change control process properly implemented to manage changes to cost, scope, schedule, or quality?

1227. How well were your expectations met regarding the extent of your involvement in the biModal IT project (effort, time commitments, etc.)?

1228. How clear were you on your role in the biModal IT project?

1229. Were quality procedures built into the biModal IT project?

1230. Overall, how effective were the efforts to prepare you and your organization for the impact of the product/service of the biModal IT project?

1231. What things surprised you on the biModal IT project that were not in the plan?

Index